Digital Fabrications

Architectural and Material Techniques

Lisa Iwamoto

Princeton Architectural Press, New York

Published by
Princeton Architectural Press
37 East Seventh Street
New York, New York 10003

For a free catalog of books, call 1.800.722.6657.
Visit our website at www.papress.com.

Project Editor: Clare Jacobson
Copy Editor: Lauren Neefe
Designer: Brett Yasko

Special thanks to: Nettie Aljian, Bree Anne Apperley, Sara Bader,
Nicola Bednarek, Janet Behning, Becca Casbon, Carina Cha,
Penny (Yuen Pik) Chu, Carolyn Deuschle, Russell Fernandez,
Pete Fitzpatrick, Wendy Fuller, Jan Haux, Aileen Kwun, Nancy
Eklund Later, Linda Lee, Laurie Manfra, John Myers, Katharine
Myers, Lauren Nelson Packard, Dan Simon, Andrew Stephanian,
Jennifer Thompson, Paul Wagner, Joseph Weston, and Deb Wood
of Princeton Architectural Press —Kevin C. Lippert, publisher

Front cover: *Technicolor Bloom*, Brennan Buch, 2007.
Photo: Christof Gaggl
Back cover: "Housing in Vienna," Matias del Campo and
Sandra Manninger/SPAN, 2007–8. Photo: SPAN
Page 1: *Voussoir Cloud*, IwamotoScott Architecture, 2008.
Photo: Joshua White

Library of Congress Cataloging-in-Publication Data
Iwamoto, Lisa, 1963–
Digital fabrications : architectural and material techniques /
Lisa Iwamoto.
p. cm. — (Architecture briefs)
Includes bibliographical references.
ISBN 978-1-56898-790-3 (alk. paper)
1. Architectural design—Data processing. 2. Architecture—
Data processing. 3. Computer-aided design. I. Title.
NA2728.I93 2009
720.285—dc22   2008029765

The Architecture Brief series takes on a variety of single topics
of interest to architecture students and young professionals.
Field-specific information and digital techniques are presented
in a user-friendly manner along with basic principles of design
and construction. The series familiarizes readers with the
concepts and technical terms necessary to successfully translate
ideas into built form.

Also available in this series:
Architects Draw: Freehand Fundamentals,
Sue Ferguson Gussow, 978-1-56898-740-8

Architectural Photography the Digital Way,
Gerry Kopelow, 978-1-56898-697-5

Building Envelopes: An Integrated Approach,
Jenny Lovell, 978-1-56898-818-4

004 Introduction

008 **Sectioning**

017 *Digital Weave*, University of California, Berkeley/Lisa Iwamoto
022 *Mafoombey*, Martti Kalliala, Esa Ruskeepää, with Martin Lukasczyk
026 *(Ply)Wood Delaminations*, Georgia Institute of Technology/Monica Ponce de Leon
028 *A Change of State*, Georgia Institute of Technology/Nader Tehrani
030 *[c]space*, Alan Dempsey and Alvin Huang
032 *BURST**.003*, SYSTEMarchitects

034 **Tessellating**

042 *West Coast Pavilion*, Atelier Manferdini
046 *Huyghe + Le Corbusier Puppet Theater*, MOS
050 *Helios House*, Office dA and Johnston Marklee & Associates
052 *California: Stage Set for John Jasperse*, AEDS/Ammar Eloueini
054 *Airspace Tokyo*, Thom Faulders Architecture
056 *Technicolor Bloom*, Brennan Buck

060 **Folding**

069 *Dragonfly*, Tom Wiscombe/EMERGENT
074 *Nubik*, AEDS/Ammar Eloueini
076 *In-Out Curtain*, IwamotoScott
078 *Entry Paradise Pavilion*, Chris Bosse/PTW Architects
080 Aoba-tei, Atelier Hitoshi Abe
082 *Digital Origami*, University of Technology, Sydney/Chris Bosse
084 *C_Wall*, Andrew Kudless/Matsys
086 *Manifold*, Andrew Kudless/Matsys

088 **Contouring**

094 *Bone Wall*, Urban A&O
098 *Design 306*, Erwin Hauer and Enrique Rosado
100 *CNC panels*, Jeremy Ficca
101 *Door with Peephole*, WILLIAMSONWILLIAMSON
102 *Gradient Scale*, SPAN
103 *Tool-Hide*, Ruy Klein

106 **Forming**

113 *Alice*, Florencia Pita mod
118 *Prototype Pavilion*, MOS
122 *UniBodies*, PATTERNS, with Kreysler & Associates
124 *NGTV*, GNUFORM
126 "Dark Places," servo
130 "Housing in Vienna," SPAN
132 *Satin Sheet*, University of California, Los Angeles/Heather Roberge
135 *Shiatsu*, University of California, Los Angeles/Heather Roberge
138 *P_Wall*, Andrew Kudless/Matsys

140 Notes
141 Project Credits

Architecture continually informs and is informed by its modes of representation and construction, perhaps never more so than now, when digital media and emerging technologies are rapidly expanding what we conceive to be formally, spatially, and materially possible. Digital fabrication, in particular, has spurred a design revolution, yielding a wealth of architectural invention and innovation. How designs use digital fabrication and material techniques to calibrate between virtual model and physical artifact is the subject of this book.

In "Translations from Drawing to Building," Robin Evans expands on the inevitable separation architects encounter between drawing, the traditional medium of design, and building, the final outcome of their work.[1] As he describes it, great invention occurs in this gap. Like traditional drawing, digital production is a generative medium that comes with its own host of restraints and possibilities. Digital practices have the potential to narrow the gap between representation and building, affording a hypothetically seamless connection between design and making. As with any design process, however, there are invariably gaps among the modes of making. And, as with all tools of production, the very techniques that open these investigations have their own sets of constraints and gear particular ways of working. In the best cases, such as those shown in this book, innovation is born out of this fissure and advances design.

Digital Fabrications: Architectural and Material Techniques documents architecturally innovative projects realized through digital design and constructive processes. By way of several ground-breaking projects, it offers a brief and informative background to the rise of digital fabrication in architecture, providing insight into why it has sparked the imagination of a new generation of designers. It also contains practical information about the types of tools and technologies architects most frequently use for digital fabrication. The bulk of the book, however, is devoted to illustrating projects that reveal the design ingenuity that arises from digital

fabrication and the material practices it has shaped and revitalized.

This book is unique because it concentrates on work designed and built by emerging and newly defined practices that, with a do-it-yourself attitude, regularly pioneer techniques and experiment with fabrication processes on a small scale. The means by which these projects were realized are within the reach of many practitioners and students. Here, the architectural project is a form of applied design research. These architects seek to leverage digital design and manufacturing for perceptual, spatial, and formal effect. The projects center on a mode of inquiry whose method of making ultimately forms the design aesthetic. Many of the practitioners teach as well and bring their interests into the classroom, offering the architecture student an opportunity to "do it" as well. For this reason, some excellent student projects have been included in the pages that follow.

The book is organized according to types of digital fabrication techniques that have emerged over the past fifteen years: sectioning, tessellating, folding, contouring, and forming. Each section introduces the basics of the featured technique through a description of pioneering case studies, after which there is a collection of projects demonstrating how architects have manipulated the tectonic method for design. Naturally, the projects overstep the chapter definitions: many combine two or three techniques. The distinctions nevertheless structure and contextualize the work, so that the projects gain specificity in light of the others.

Lastly, this book aims to show both working method and final results, documenting working drawings, templates, and material prototypes. Books on digital design tend to be highly technical, focused on documenting a few large building projects in great detail or else speculating more broadly on the implications of digital fabrication for the future of the profession. Missing from these efforts is a visually exciting collection of smaller built projects focused on design. *Digital Fabrications* does just that and will be of interest to anyone who wants to know how digital fabrication works, why architects use it, and how it promotes innovative design.

Background

It is inconceivable today to imagine designing buildings without the use of computers. They are used at every step of the architectural process, from conceptual design to construction. Three-dimensional modeling and visualization, generative form finding, scripted modulation systems, structural and thermal analyses, project management and coordination, and file-to-factory production are just some of the digital practices employed by architects and building consultants. Digital fabrication is often one of the final stages of this process, and it is very much what it sounds like: a way of making that uses digital data to control a fabrication process. Falling under the umbrella of computer-aided design and manufacturing (CAD/CAM), it relies on computer-driven machine tools to build or cut parts.

CAD/CAM has been a mainstay of industrial design and engineering and of manufacturing industries—particularly the automotive and aerospace industries—for more than a half century. Parts ranging from engine blocks to cell phones are designed and built using 3D-computer-modeling software. Scaled models are made quickly, using rapid-prototyping machines that turn out accurate physical models from the computerized data. Once the computer model is refined and completed, the data are transferred to computer-controlled machines that make full-scale parts and molds from a range of materials such as aluminum, steel, wood, and plastics. This computerized process streamlines production—effectively blending upstream and downstream processes that are typically compartmentalized, often eliminating intermediate steps between design and final production. There is the potential for architecture also to move more fluidly between design and construction. As Branko Kolarevic states, "This newfound ability to generate construction information directly from design information, and not the complex curving forms, is what defines the most profound aspect of much of the contemporary architecture."[2]

Architects have been drawing digitally for nearly thirty years. CAD programs have made two-dimensional drawing efficient, easy to edit, and, with a little practice, simple to do. Yet for many years, as the process of making drawings steadily shifted from being analog to digital, the design of buildings did not really reflect the change. CAD replaced drawing with a parallel rule and lead pointer, but buildings looked pretty much the same. This is perhaps not so surprising—one form of two-dimensional representation simply replaced another. It took three-dimensional-computer modeling and digital fabrication to energize design thinking and expand the boundaries of architectural form and construction.

In a relatively short period of time, a network of activities has grown up around digital fabrication. Inventive methods have emerged from project-specific applications developed by a handful of architects and fabricators. This inventiveness has to do in part with restructuring the very process of construction. The work of Gehry Partners and its associated firm Gehry Technologies has played a pivotal role in this regard. For them, digital integration was largely necessitated by the complexity of the building geometries.

Gehry's office began using CAD/CAM processes in 1989 to develop and then test the constructability of a building system for the Disney Concert Hall. As is usually the case in design, the process was iterative and nonlinear. Initially, physical models were reverse-engineered using a digitizer to take coordinates off a model's surface and import it into a 3D digital environment. The design subsequently moved back and forth between physical and digital surface models—physical models for aesthetics, digital models for "system fit." For this purpose Gehry's office adapted software from the aerospace industry, CATIA (Computer Aided Three Dimensional Interactive Application), to model the entire exterior of the concert hall.[3] At that time the skin was conceived as stone and glass, and the office successfully produced cut-stone mock-ups, using tool paths for computer-controlled milling machines derived from digital surface models. In other words, the digital model was translated directly into physical production by using digitally driven machines that essentially sculpted the stone surface through the cutting away of material. This building method revealed that the complexities and uniqueness of surface geometries did not significantly affect fabrication costs, and it is this realization, that one can make a series of unique pieces with nearly the same effort as it requires to mass-produce identical ones, that forms a significant aspect of the computer-aided manufacturing that has since been exploited for design effect.

In 2002, Gehry Partners created Gehry Technologies to further develop Digital Project, a version of CATIA adapted and specialized for the unique demands of complex architectural projects. Digital Project integrates numerous aspects of the construction process, including building codes, and mechanical, structural, and cost-criteria aspects. Gehry Technologies now acts as a consultant to Gehry Partners, as well as to other architects, assisting with digital construction and management. The company is revolutionary in that it expands the role of the architect to include oversight of the building and construction-management process, much as it was in the age of the master builder. In addition to Gehry's, architectural offices such as Foster & Partners, Nicholas Grimshaw, and Bernhard Franken are forging similar integrated project-delivery methods for large, complex projects. The focus of this book, however, is less on integration with the construction industry and more on another avenue of investigation taken by architects relative to digital fabrication: design-build experimentation at a one-to-one scale.

Recent Experimentation
We have experienced a fertile generation of architecture focused on the expanding possibilities of material and formal production. Digital methods have fundamentally shifted the discipline of

architecture, and many paths now characterize this design arena. The architects included here are committed to employing the fluid potentials of technology to inform the design process and gear the evolution of their designs, while their experimentation is remarkable for being on a one-to-one scale. This approach recognizes what Michael Speaks has termed "design intelligence": "Making becomes knowledge or intelligence creation. In this way thinking and doing, design and fabrication, and prototype and final design become blurred, interactive, and part of a non-linear means of innovation."[4] As it does for the large-scale work of Frank Gehry and others, the digital environment allows architects to take control of the building process. Several groundbreaking projects helped instigate this avenue of design research and shape a new generation of architects.

Within a span of about five years beginning in the mid-1990s, a host of projects appeared that clearly demonstrated the aesthetic merits of using digital devices. These include, among others, William Massie's concrete formwork, Greg Lynn's waffle typologies, and Bernard Cache's surface manipulations, all of which will be discussed at greater length in the chapter introductions. In seeing these projects, one cannot deny that, in addition to the professional, industrial, and economic benefits associated with CAD/CAM, building with the computer achieves unprecedented visual, material, and formal results. While the ingenuity of the following projects goes far beyond the outward appearance, the strong visual aspect nevertheless plays a significant role in sparking the imagination of young designers. These early projects are the achievement most notably of architects with material know-how and a will to experiment—traits that have now increasingly permeated design culture.

To move from design to construction, it is necessary to translate graphical data from two-dimensional drawings and three-dimensional models into digital data that a computer-numeric-controlled (CNC) machine can understand. This demands that architects essentially learn a new language. Some aspects of this translation are relatively automatic and involve using machine-specific software; others are very much in the purview of design. Decisions as to which machine and method to use must marry design intent with machine capability. It has therefore become necessary for digitally savvy architects to understand how these tools work, what materials they are best suited for, and where in the tooling process the possibilities lie.

Along these lines, architects have begun to couple form with method and revisit tectonic systems as a means to produce material effect. They seek to elevate standard building materials perceptually through nonstandard fabrication processes. Surfaces form buildings, and they can do so through smooth, undifferentiated expanses, or they can be constructed, textured, assembled, patterned, ornamented, or otherwise articulated. Digital fabrication opens onto a sea of possibilities. Punching, laser cutting, water-jet cutting, CNC routing, and die cutting are just some of the automated processes fueling this design domain.

Practically speaking, because buildings are made from a series of parts, their assembly relies on techniques of aggregating and manipulating two-dimensional materials. Computer fabrication has opened a realm for architects to perceptually heighten and make visible the nature of this accretion through constructed repetition and difference. The subtle variation of a system of elements, the transformation of recognizable materials, and the visceral response, no less, to viewing the result of intensive material accumulation—often understood to be the purview of the low arts or crafts—have been digitally redefined into a vocabulary by which architectural language is transformed. The projects shown in this book expand on these digital production techniques and capitalize on material methods as a generator for design. The architects here are concerned both with tectonics of assembly and with synthetic surface and material effect. The results are extraordinary—intricate patterns, filtered light, or evocations of abstracted images at mural scale—and all achieved through the aggregation of simple building materials.

The following chapters discuss architects who have honed digital-fabrication techniques on specific projects. Each discussion is accompanied by a detailed breakdown of the fabrication technique, providing insight into the recent projects featured in each chapter. These are projects that concentrate on the fertile realm of one-to-one-scale experimentation, which demands reciprocity between design and empirical innovation. The final outcomes hinge on the ability to reconcile the developmental shifts in material and working method. While the individual projects naturally take on different emphases, the work consistently elucidates provocative liaisons between digital production and making. Compelling design projects in and of themselves, they are both testaments to smaller-scale experimentation and the testing grounds for buildings to come.

Martti Kalliala, Esa Ruskeepää, Martin Lukasczyk, *Mafoombey*, elevation detail.
Photo: Martti Kalliala, Esa Ruskeepää with Martin Lukasczyk

Sectioning

Orthographic projections—that is, plans and sections—are one of the most valuable representational tools architects have at their disposal. They are an indispensable communication and design device. They have also contributed to a prominent digital fabrication method. With computer modeling, deriving sections is no longer a necessarily two-dimensional drawing exercise. In fact, it is no longer an exercise in projection at all but a process of taking cuts through a formed three-dimensional object. As architects increasingly design with complex geometries, using sectioning as a method of taking numerous cross sections through a form has proven time and again an effective and compelling technique. As in conventional construction processes, information is translated from one format to another to communicate with the builder—only in this case the builder is a machine.

Rather than construct the surface itself, sectioning uses a series of profiles, the edges of which follow lines of surface geometry. The modeling software's sectioning or contouring commands can almost instantaneously cut parallel sections through objects at designated intervals. This effectively streamlines the process of making serialized, parallel sections. Architects have experimented with sectional assemblies as a way to produce both surface and structure.

While it is distinctly within the domain of digital techniques, sectioning has a long history in the construction industry. It is commonly used in airplane and shipbuilding to make the doubly curving surfaces associated with their respective built forms. Objects such as airplane bodies and boat hulls are first defined sectionally as a series of structural ribs, then clad with a surface material. Lofting—the method that determines the shape of the cladding or surface panels by building between curved cross-sectional profiles—is analogous to lofting in digital software. Lofted surfaces can be unrolled into flat pieces or else geometrically redescribed in section as curves along the surface.

This building technique was adopted in the predigital era by architects such as Le Corbusier. The roof of the chapel at Ronchamp, for example—likened to an airplane wing by the architect—is designed and built as a series of structural concrete ribs, tied together laterally by crossbeams. A paper model of the roof clearly shows the intentions for the internal construction. The advantages of using this type of hollow construction are clear: it is a lightweight structure that provides accurate edge profiles for a nonuniform shape on which to align and support surface material, in this case thin shells of concrete. In his book *Ronchamp*, Le Corbusier enumerates the unique constructional makeup in a manner that recalls the makeup of digitally constructed projects: "Seven strong, flat beams, 17 cm. thick, all different."[1]

Another architect who worked almost exclusively with forms that required nonstandard construction was Frederick Kiesler. Indeed he has become a poster child of sorts for protoblob architecture. In the context of digital fabrication, his relevance has less to do with the shapes of his buildings and more to do with his efforts to develop a method for building his "endless" forms. It is not surprising that Kiesler's endeavors in this regard have correlations with digital construction. Although the truly organic form of his Endless House was never realized, he did complete several projects, most notably Peggy Guggenheim's Art of This Century gallery, in 1942. The gallery bespeaks his desire for a sentient architecture that would be responsive to its occupants' mercurial perceptions: the picture frames are suspended from the walls so as to interact with various viewers against a curved backdrop. Study sketches of the curved wall and ceiling reveal sectional ribs that are aestheticized to resemble an airplane or other machined framework. The curvature of the wall is consistent along its length, so, unlike the ribs of Le Corbusier's chapel at Ronchamp, these are repetitive. What is similar about these projects is their employment of sectioning for constructional and geometric purposes in the making of curved forms.

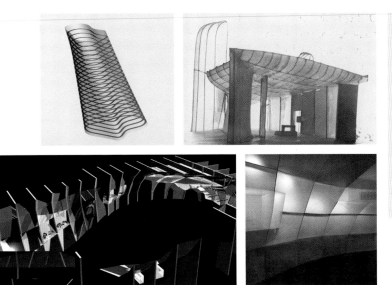

Example of cutting sections using contour command in Rhinoceros. Photo: L. Iwamoto

Le Corbusier, Chapelle Notre Dame du Haut de Ronchamp, 1950. Scaled model showing ribbed roof structure. © FLC/ARS, 2008. Courtesy Fondation Le Corbusier

Greg Lynn, Artists Space installation, Artists Space, New York, 1995. Final installation showing lights behind Mylar panels. Photo: Greg Lynn/Form

Artists Space installation. Rendering of sectional ribs. Photo: Greg Lynn/Form

Rather than expose the constructional system, however, the sectioning in both cases is a substrate for the application of a surface material and the achievement of a smooth finished form.

Greg Lynn was one of the first to experiment with digitally generated sectional construction as part of a highly influential design methodology. In his 1999 book *Animate Form*, Lynn formulates an architectural approach out of the emergence of dynamic forces, flows, and organizations. By harnessing the computer's potential as a generative medium for design, he asserts, there are "distinct formal and visual consequences of the use of computer animation. For instance, the most obvious aesthetic consequence is the shift from volumes defined by Cartesian coordinates to topological surfaces defined by U and V vector coordinates."[2] This revelation ushered in a whole new mode of formally and organizationally fluid, digitally driven design.

Animate Form catalogs the projects Lynn uses as examples of animate architecture. Four of these projects were featured, with evocatively glowing stereolithography models, in a solo exhibition at Artists Space, in New York, in 1995. Yet it was the very construction of the exhibition that is in the domain of digital fabrication. Lynn designed the installation to push his process toward full-scale construction. Whereas he derived the design itself from a dynamic process of nodal interaction, he relied on simple planar material for its construction. Initially the form was curvilinear, made of parallel sectioned ribs cut from a plastic sheet using two-dimensional computer plots as full-scale cutting templates. The ribs were faced with triangulated Mylar panels to make a continuous volume. Both the translation of the original volume into a sectioned grid and the approximation of the originally smooth shell as a tessellated surface resulted from the mandates of full-scale construction. Yet rather than produce a partial representation of what should have been a curvilinear form, the constructional imperatives created an articulated system for display.

William Massie, another pioneer in digital construction, designed a series of installations based on sectioning. *Playa Urbana/Urban Beach*, Massie's winning design for MoMA/P.S.1's Young Architects Program courtyard installation in 2002, revisits the spanning of surface material and offers a new version of this constructional system. It has translated the

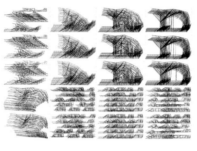

CLOCKWISE FROM TOP LEFT:

William Massie, *Playa Urbana/Urban Beach*, MoMA/P.S.1, Queens, New York, 2002. Photo: William Massie

Playa Urbana/Urban Beach. Detail of steel rib. Photo: William Massie

SHoP Architects, *Dunescape*, 2001. Plot files of cross sections used for construction layout. Photo: SHoP Architects

Dunescape. Installation. Photo: SHoP Architects

system into laser-cut steel fins threaded with exposed PVC tubing, creating the effect of diaphanous surfaces of flowing plastic hair that create shade and accommodate program. The sensuous lines are a constructive solution that cumulatively define the larger surfaces and representationally echo the digital method that made them. That is, the lines define the physical surface in the same way that embedded surface curves, or isoparms, make up a digitally ruled, or lofted, one.

Massie's method coordinates well with conventional building materials. Standard materials typically come as sheets, so that three-dimensional buildings are made from two-dimensional materials. In the case of sectioning, the constructional techniques that have emerged include sectional ribbing (as in the projects already described), lamination or parallel stacking, and waffle-grid construction. In the case of parallel stacking, the frequency of the sections required to approximate the increasingly varied surface geometries increases, sometimes resulting in a visual intensification of material. By using edge profiles to describe surface through implied visual continuities, architects have

taken advantage of sectioning—both to merge and to perceptually elevate the relationship of form with material tectonic.

A good example of this merging and perceptual elevation is *Dunescape*, the project that won MoMA/ P.S.1's Young Architects Program the year before Massie's *Playa Urbana/Urban Beach*. Designed and built by by SHoP Architects, *Dunescape* is an architecturalized landscape built completely as a series of parallel, stacked dimensional lumber. While manual labor was required to cut, assemble, and fasten the pieces in the actual construction, the methodology was completely digitally driven. First, the digital model was sectioned at intervals that were established by the given material thickness. The resulting section drawings were then plotted at full scale and used as templates on which to lay out and position each wood piece. Not insignificantly, SHoP used this very same technique to make a scaled model in the digital file submitted for the competition presentation—a convincing testament to this particular technique's fluidity, scalability, and credibility.

The substantial rhetoric that has surrounded digital fabrication toward the streamlining of

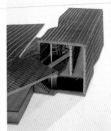

construction practice is certainly warranted. Computerized two-and-a-half- and three-axis cutting tools—such as laser cutters, CNC routers, water-jet and plasma cutters—all work from the same polylines to cut two-dimensional materials. While the scale and thickness and size of material may change, the files used to communicate with the various pieces of equipment work off the same set of profiles. Early adopters made a conceptual leap to bridge digital and physical model making with full-scale construction. The leap has yielded a wealth of compelling and sophisticated architectural explorations that have advanced forms of three-dimensional representation and building.

Laser cutters in particular have facilitated the conceptual and practical move from making models to executing full-scale construction. Most laser cutters are small; most typically work with model-making materials such as chipboard, acrylic, and cardboard; and most are easy to use with familiar software such as AutoCAD and Adobe Illustrator. Initially laser cutters were employed by architects for precision model making, as for engraved building facades, structural members, and building details. Later

coupling these machines with the digital-design software that fostered nonstandard form making and came equipped with commands to redescribe those precision forms through serial sections, designers were soon able to envision how sectioning, as a representational method, could become a building technique.

Preston Scott Cohen's *House on a Terminal Line* (1998), for example, conceptually unites ground and house by employing a technique of waffle construction for both. Conceived as an inflected landscape, the project was made by taking the perpendicular intersection of two sets of parallel sections through the whole digital model. The planes meet at corresponding notches, resulting in a gridded, wafflelike framework. Waffle construction is by no means new: such common items as old-fashioned metal ice trays and fluorescent-light baffles have used intersecting grids for years. Though not ultimately built, this project nevertheless provides insight into how the technique could be used for construction as well. In 2001, the Paris-based firm Jakob + MacFarlane used waffle construction as the foundation for the design and construction of the Loewy Bookshop.

The technique is well suited to the programs of shelving and storage and to using readily available sheet materials. Other such projects by other firms have followed, making waffle construction somewhat ubiquitous in the lexicon of digital fabrication, yet it retains its power as a supple technique because of its inherent ability to be adapted and modulated for a multiplicity of forms. Likewise, as a constructional system, it can accommodate projects of multiple scales and work with a range of building materials.

A recent project that notably refined the grid shell was the Serpentine Gallery Pavilion 2005, by Álvaro Siza and Eduardo Souto de Moura, with structural engineering by Cecil Balmond. The waffle grid is revisioned as a nonstandard lamella truss. The large single-span, low-vaulted enclosure was made by connecting small interdependent pieces with a mortise-and-tenon connection in an overlapping skewed grid pattern. Each of the 427 timber pieces had a unique profile, mapped from thirty-six control points that were derived using a computer script. These rib geometries were sent digitally to the timber fabricators, who cut each piece using a five-axis CNC mill.[3] Like masonry vaults, the drapelike roof is initially supported by extensive shoring; when the form is completed, all the members can lock together in compression. Unlike more typical waffle construction, which relies on continuous ribs, this structure is based on an aggregation of mutually dependent pieces. Each piece can be lifted and placed by one or two people, which substantially simplifies the construction process. In keeping with Siza and Souto de Moura's initial intent for an Arte Povera structure, the pavilion is built in a handmade, low-tech manner that is nonetheless enabled by the precision of high-tech machinery.

Another good example of a modified waffle is [c]space, the competition-winning pavilion designed and built for the Architectural Association by Alan Dempsey and Alvin Huang. The sectioning takes into account the continuously changing curvature of the shell-like form, and, unlike grid shells, the ribs

in both directions are discontinuous, resulting in an atypical, less hierarchical structural performance.

At a much larger scale, Herzog & de Meuron's Bird's Nest expands the vocabulary of sectioning, drawing out its potential for informality and irregularity. Unlike typical sectioning or waffle construction, which relies on parallel planes of material, the structure of Bird's Nest is defined by revolving diagonal sections. Diagonal sectioning simply involves a rotation of the cutting plane nonorthogonally to either the longitudinal or transverse building geometry. In this case, the sections are taken tangentially to the oblong center ring of the nestlike form, creating an overlapping pattern that becomes the primary truss structure. Additional lines are similarly geometrically derived from sections through the overall form and become secondary structure and circulation. The building scale demands that each member is not a single material but built up into large box beams whose construction relies on digital data to define the geometries and which are manually assembled by a large labor force.

Diagonal grid construction is also integral to the execution of the BURST* house by SYSTEMarchitects. The BURST* house is made using a customizable kit of parts, whereby "the bulk of the construction process is achieved on the computer, where the geometry of the house and the individual pieces— structural ribs, walls, floors—are resolved and then sent to be precisely cut and numbered, before being delivered to the site. This reduces the assembly process to a more accessible process of simple fitting together, much like a jigsaw puzzle with pre-labeled pieces."[4] The house is composed of shells in which the diagonal waffle and diamond-shaped cladding form what the architects call a "structural weave." Because the pattern of the ribs is at an acute diagonal, the members are not notched together but joined at each intersection with bent metal plates. This system maintains the structural integrity of the diaphragm while breaking each rib into smaller segments for easier handling.

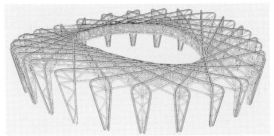

Sectioning as a technique for building has also evolved for smaller projects. In some cases, the ready availability of visual images and digital processes associated with sectioning produces expected results; in others, the technique is expanded by a desire to capitalize on both tectonic and material properties. One such project is *Mafoombey*, a structured space for experiencing music and a competition-winning installation, designed by Helsinki University of Technology students Martti Kalliala and Esa Ruskeepää with the help of their friend Martin Lukasczyk. One of the most compelling aspects of the project is its economy. Stacking typically uses more material to make a volume than it would simply to build the enclosing surfaces. In the case of *Mafoombey*, however, the design of the sections negotiates material thickness with inhabitation, program, and acoustical performance. The internal geometries include cuts made for electronic equipment and depressions for the human body. Like cardboard furniture such as Frank Gehry's Easy Edges series, these students' installation is an instance of aesthetically elevating an inexpensive material through atypical construction. The thinness of the cardboard relative to the overall size of the volume enables each plane to take on a subtly different shape, which creates the visually smooth and voluptuous interior.

Sectioning readily allows for constructing such digitally generated form. However geometrically complex, the physical corollary can closely approximate the digital model through the use of appropriately scaled materials. The alignment between 3D model and constructed end is one of the great advantages of digital fabrication and its expanded application, called building information modeling (BIM).

Buildings are typically meant to correspond to the drawings that anticipate them. Rarely is it intended that the final product take a form different from the planned design. Nevertheless, the route from virtual to actual is one of constant calibration. Material behavior, gravity, construction sequencing, weather, available tools, and numerous other concerns necessarily play a part in determining the realization of built form. Taking such exigencies into account, one may observe a host of exciting digital-fabrication projects that have cropped up, using material and constructive constraints to alter end results. Because the nature of designing in such a manner is improvisational, a good portion of this one-to-one-scale digital-fabrication research is conducted at academic institutions, by students under the guidance of young practitioners and professors. In this context, relationships among the design, material, fabrication, and assembly are intentionally kept flexible through the final building stage. The design-build process fosters experimentation, where fortuitous "accidents" may lead to new insights and unintended design consequences.

As Georgia Tech's Ventulett Distinguished Chairs in Architectural Design, Office dA principals Monica Ponce de Leon and Nader Tehrani led a series of studios from 2004 to 2006 that examined the productive conflicts between digital design and material assembly. The studios culminated in full-scale installations made by teams of students.

One of the 2005 projects, *(Ply)wood Delaminations*, takes the technique of straightforward parallel sectioning as its starting point. Strands of CNC-routed plywood cascade down the multistory atrium at Georgia Tech's College of Architecture building, splitting off at intermediate floors and at the ground floor to make seating. Where projects like *Mafoombey* use consecutive stacking to provide a solid structure, *(Ply)wood Delaminations* widely spaces the largely vertical ribs to make a porous surface. The constructive challenge is to maintain the continuity of a large surface that is composed of short, separate pieces. For the most part, the ribs are kept at an even distance by steel rods, threaded through precut holes to regulate the spacing. The pliability of wood and the natural tendency of long strips of material to deflect are celebrated toward the bottom of the installation, where the members are pinched together to create an informal array of elongated eye-shaped openings. These add a new dimension to the overall structure at a scale between the material part and the overall form. *A Change of State*, a project completed the following year under Tehrani, extends the dialogue of flexible materials and digital construction. This design literally moves from a stacked, striated condition at one end to a loose organization of pillowing strips at the other, using the inherent flexibility of plastic to achieve the formal effect.

Digital Weave, an installation designed and built in 2004 by my own graduate students at the University of California, Berkeley, similarly adapted a sectional methodology to a pliable material. The design was begun by making a simple digital model that was sectioned in a radial fashion into vertical ribs. The rib profiles were then refined to correspond to full-scale construction prototypes. Early in the design process, mock-ups of collapsible systems were made to test constructability and structural stability. The accordion-like structure was then made by slicing each rib longitudinally with dashed cuts and pulling it apart in an alternating rhythm. The final design uses clear acrylic compression rods to expand the ribs and give shape to the overall volume. The ribs are held in place through compression and friction and are easily removed for demounting and transportation. Although the students sought geometric alliances between the digital profiles and full-scale mock-ups, the end product was ultimately the result of allowing material deformations to shape the form.

In negotiating constructive exigencies, the project illustrates the adoption of now well-established steps for translating sectional cuts into a material system. Because the sectional cuts are not parallel to one another, the ribs are first rotated, moved onto a consistent plane, and consecutively labeled. Unlike the spacing of the ribs in *Mafoombey*, the wide spacing of the ribs in *Digital Weave* results in each rib's being significantly different from the next. The ribs are attached with rivets at connections that alternate between the inside and outside edges, demanding that each match its neighbor along one side. Therefore, each rib was redrawn to have a unique profile that slightly reshaped the overall form. Students worked in AutoCAD to refine the rib geometries, to introduce the internal football-shaped holes that allowed for the ribs to spread, and to draw all the rivet holes. The ribs were then laid on four-by-eight-foot templates to match the corrugated plastic sheet material and fabricated using a CNC water-jet cutter. The subsequent assembly proceeded rapidly as each rib came off the water-jet cutter, ready to be riveted together in groups of ten for easy transportation and breakdown. Finally, the ribs that had been slipped into the slots in the plywood floor were expanded using the compression rods and then were bolted together on-site.

The projects in this chapter demonstrate the ample diversity of sectioning as a construction technique. There is an eloquent simplicity to the stacked, layered, and gridded tectonic that opens the door to wide constructional interpretation. Ultimately, it is the defamiliarization of both method and material that allows each project to transcend the linear translation from digital to physical sectioning. The intermediary calibration is what ensures that the architects have virtually limitless possibilities for design.

Digital Weave
University of California, Berkeley/Lisa Iwamoto, 2004

Digital Weave was designed for the San Francisco Museum of Modern Art Contemporary Extension (SFMOMA CX). The project had the constraint of extreme temporality: it was shown for one night only, and it had to be installed and de-installed on-site in a matter of hours. The design engages in constructional and material investigations of creating an architecture for such a transitory condition. The project utilizes CAD/CAM techniques as a conceptual and constructional strategy to meet the strict time constraints.

Digital Weave was completed in a five-week design-build segment of a graduate design studio at the University of California, Berkeley. It was conceived as a kit of parts, such that the detail becomes the whole, and it is designed as a concertina-like structure that can be compressed to a fraction of the size. This compressible aspect drove the design, since the thirty-two-by-eighteen-by-eleven-foot-high volume needed to be installed in such a short period of time.

The wrapped volume forms two semi-enclosed interior lounge spaces. It is constructed from a series of woven ribs, which are made by riveting together aluminum plates that are sandwiched around an inexpensive translucent corrugated plastic sign material. The ribs slot into a puzzle-like plywood floor. All the pieces are fabricated digitally with a computer-controlled water-jet cutter. The precision afforded by this technology enables the pieces to fit together smoothly without any mechanical fasteners other than those used for the ribs. The desire to create an atmosphere larger than the allotted installation space was achieved through projection. The ephemeral yet intricate nature of the project also manifested a unique atmosphere.

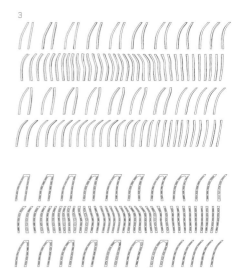

UC Berkeley students with Lisa Iwamoto, *Digital Weave*, 2004.

1 Rhinoceros model of overall surface enclosure.

2 Section cuts shown in plan.

3 Ribs extracted and translated into AutoCAD. Original rib profiles and adjusted profiles in red match adjacent rib edge.

4 Rib profiles laid out on four-by-eight-foot templates for water-jet cutting.

5 Final full-scale mock-up.

6 Full-scale mock-up testing acrylic compression struts.

7 Water-jet cutting at Lawrence Berkeley National Laboratory Design and Engineering shop.

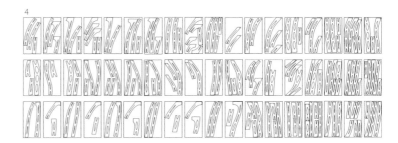

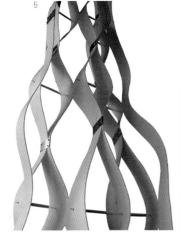

8 Assembly of ribs into expanding accordion-like system.
9 Portion of woven rib surface expanded using acrylic compression struts.
10 Trial setup of *Digital Weave* in studio at UC Berkeley.
11 Plan of floor divided into sections for transportation.
12 Floor sections laid out on four-by-eight-foot templates for water-jet cutting.
13 Detail of floor edge with slots to insert ribs.
14 Floor assembly.
15 Project assembly.

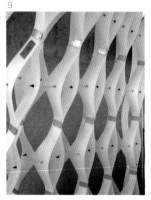

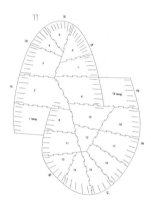

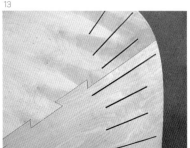

Photo: Timo Wright

Mafoombey
**Martti Kalliala, Esa Ruskeepää,
with Martin Lukasczyk, 2005**

Mafoombey was the winning entry in a design contest arranged by the University of Art and Design in Helsinki in 2005. The competition brief called for a space for listening and experiencing music within the set dimensions of two and a half cubic meters. The project was executed with 3D software and scale models.

The design builds up from a simple architectural concept: a free-form cavernous space that is cut into a cubic volume of stacked material. The low resolution of form and the perception of weight achieved through a layered structure were determined to be the key issues. Research into various materials suggested corrugated cardboard as optimal for its low cost and excellent acoustics. Furthermore, the material has a strong aesthetic appeal, which the designers felt had not been fully exploited at the scale of the project.

Mafoombey consists of 360 layers of seven-millimeter corrugated cardboard, adding up to 720 half-square sheets. The sheets, 2.5 meters by 1.25 meters, are cut one by one using a computer-controlled cutter. The structure sits under its own dead weight without fixing. The lightweight assembly details ensure relatively easy transportation and quick construction.

ABOVE: **Assembly and finished exterior.** Photos: Timo Wright
BELOW: **Program and equipment void diagram sections.**

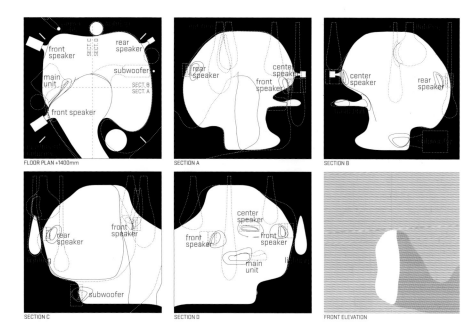

FLOOR PLAN +1400mm

SECTION A

SECTION B

SECTION C

SECTION D

FRONT ELEVATION

Photo: Jukka Uotila

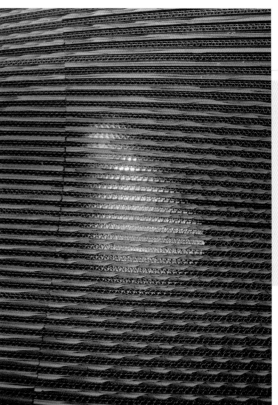

ABOVE: **Detail of surface.** Photo: Timo Wright
LEFT: Section templates.
BELOW: Axonometric diagram of interior voids.

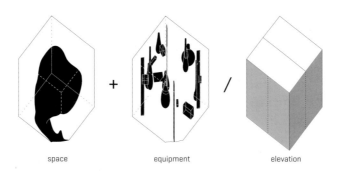

space   +   equipment   /   elevation

LEFT: View from second-floor mezzanine.
OPPOSITE TOP: Installation.
OPPOSITE BELOW LEFT: CNC-milled lap joints.
OPPOSITE BELOW RIGHT: Diagram of lap joint.
All photos: Phil Jones

(Ply)wood Delaminations
Georgia Institute of Technology/
Monica Ponce de Leon, 2005

(Ply)wood Delaminations is one result of a digital design-build course taught at Georgia Tech by Monica Ponce de Leon during her tenure as the Ventulett Distinguished Chair in Architectural Design in 2005. The projects that came out of the course took advantage of one of the school's unique resources: the Advanced Wood Products Laboratory. The lab features a large collection of CNC equipment, which is intended to provide researchers with the means to expand the use of wood products. *(Ply)wood Delaminations* addresses the extreme vertical space

of the school's central atrium while delaminating at certain floors to provide structure and to create program, such as seating. The scheme as a whole delaminates in section, while stitching together in elevation. The lapped joints provide for a relatively seamless and strong shear connection. Each piece, including the bolt holes and the recessed, lapped face, is confined to a four-by-eight-foot sheet of plywood, and all are nested together and milled using the laboratory's CNC router.

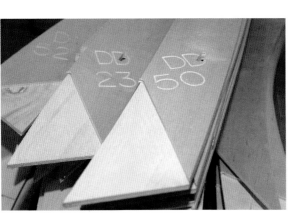

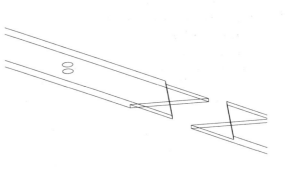

A Change of State
Georgia Institute of Technology/Nader Tehrani, 2006

This installation is the result of a one-year research process conducted by Nader Tehrani with a core team of students during his time as the Ventulett Distinguished Chair in Architectural Design at Georgia Tech. The task of the project was to analyze and develop a three-dimensional installation whose fabrication method was limited to a two-dimensional material. The underlying mission, therefore, was to radicalize the potentials of sheet material by provoking it to take on structural, spatial, programmatic, and phenomenal dimensions while adopting techniques that bring this variety of agendas into organic alignment. From the perspective of technique, the most important aspect of this project was the awareness that two-dimensional surfaces gain access to a third by way of the ruled surface.

Of the various contingencies informing the installation, the structural imperative played the most salient role. The idea was to develop a technique that could seamlessly navigate among normative structural typologies through a transformable geometric code. The aim of this geometric code was to accommodate difference within a continuous logic. The logic of the geometric unit, then, was based on the introduction and elimination of vertices—in combination with surface rotation—to create transformations in the structure. In this way, a strategy of creating phase changes was developed, imitating the way H_2O can undergo transitions from water to ice, steam, or snow.

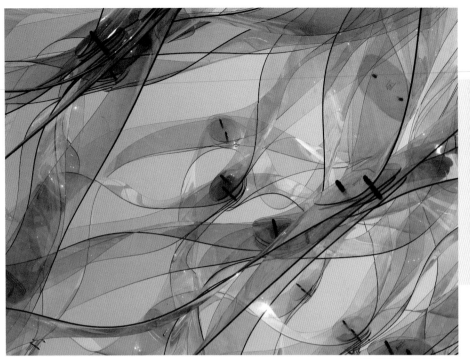

ABOVE: Detail of connections.
BELOW: Final installation showing transition
from stacked to expanded system.

All photos: Valerie Bennett

[c]space
Alan Dempsey and Alvin Huang, 2008

This pavilion was designed and constructed as part of the tenth-anniversary celebration of the Architectural Association's Design Research Laboratory. The competition brief called for an innovative structure that would utilize thirteen-millimeter-thick fiber-reinforced-concrete panels, normally used as a cladding material but employed here structurally to create a temporary ten-by-ten-by-five-meter pavilion.

The pavilion is a discontinuous shell structure, spanning more than ten meters of thin fiber-reinforced-concrete elements, which perform as structure and skin, floor walls and furniture. The design takes the material to new technical limits, having required extensive prototyping and material testing during the development phase. The jointing of discrete concrete profiles exploits the tensile strength of [fibre-C] concrete, and a simple intersecting notch joint is locked together using a bespoke rubber-gasket assembly. The angle of intersection at each joint varies continuously across the structure.

The entire design process was executed with 3D digital and physical modeling, while the development phase was completed using rigorous constraint modeling and scripting to control more than 850 distinct profiles and two thousand joints. The elements were finally manufactured directly from digital models, using CNC cutting equipment and standard thirteen-millimeter-thick flat sheets of [fibre-C] concrete and fifteen-millimeter-thick mild steel plate.

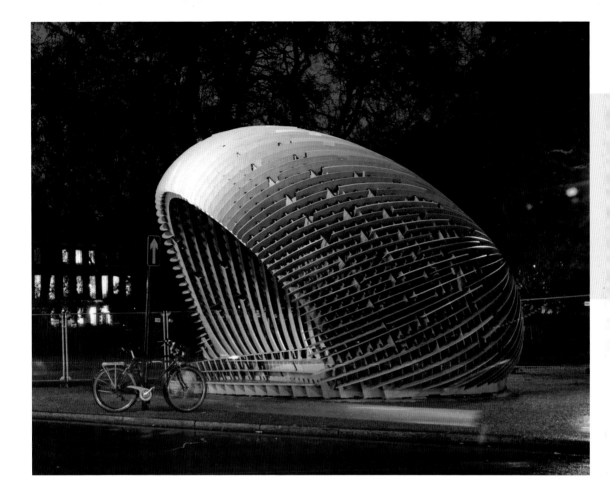

ABOVE: Plan. BELOW: Digital model describing continuous and discontinuous ribs. Analysis: Adams Kara Taylor

All photos: floto+warner studio

BURST*.003
SYSTEMarchitects, 2006

BURST* is a prefabricated system of housing that functions like a kit of parts. It produces homes that use building pieces to achieve individually tailored spaces and masses and to allow the architectural shape to conform to the specifics of distinct constraints. An alternative to the mass-produced versions of domestic life that reduce prefab housing to varied arrangements of boxes, each BURST* house has the potential for unique spaces and forms, depending on the environment, site, orientation, and the wants and requirements of the owners. The BURST* prefabrication solution is capable of adjusting to the biases of each project and each owner precisely because it uses computer technologies to expand the range of architectural form for domestic and inexpensive construction.

The bulk of the construction process is achieved on the computer, where the geometry of the house and the individual pieces—structural ribs, walls, floors—are resolved. They are then sent to be precisely cut and numbered before being delivered to the site. This method reduces the assembly to a more accessible process, much like that of a jigsaw puzzle, of simply fitting together prelabeled pieces. Once on-site, the parts can be connected by unskilled laborers in a relatively short period of time. This works not unlike a barn raising: the structural ribs are delivered to the site and then literally raised up in place to form the frame of the house.

The BURST* system is founded in the belief that prefabrication is at the scale of the construction, not at the scale of the building. The combination of precision cutting and connective knot transforms the nature of the building components themselves, as well as their assembly and relationship to one another. The BURST* housing system has picked up these two strains—precision-cut plywood and accurate connection points—to allow the frame to be woven together. This nuanced constructional system is sensitive enough to deal with and engage contemporary criteria that are in near-constant flux.

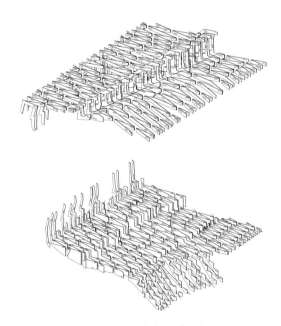

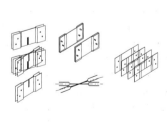

LEFT: Diagrams of constructional and wrapped surface systems.
RIGHT: Diagram of diagonal connection detail.

MOS, *Huyghe + Le Corbusier Puppet Theater*, Carpenter Center for the
Visual Arts, Cambridge, Massachusetts, 2004. Photo: Michael Vahrenwald

Tessellating

Tessellation is a collection of pieces that fit together without gaps to form a plane or surface. Tessellations can be virtually any shape so long as they puzzle together in tight formation. The geometrically patterned drawings of M.C. Escher are often cited as an example of tessellation. In architecture, the term refers to both tiled patterns on buildings and digitally defined mesh patterns.

Tessellation can be seen the world over from mosaics in ancient Rome and those of the Byzantine Empire to the screen walls in Islamic architecture or the stained-glass windows in Gothic cathedrals. These decorative surfaces were used to filter light or view, define space, or convey symbolic meaning through an abstracted notational language, much the way tessellated surfaces are used in architecture today. Because these early examples were handcrafted, overall patterns were typically achieved by laboriously assembling many small pieces into a coherent design or image. It was a time-intensive enterprise, but this aggregative technique fostered vast figural, imagistic, tonal, and geometric variation.

Digital technologies have revitalized the design world's interest in patterning and tessellation because they afford greater variation and modulation through nonstandard manufacturing, even as they provide an inherent economy of means. Working digitally enables movement from one representational format to another—for example, from digital model to vector-line file to manufacturing method. This series of translations allows for a more fluid fabrication process while significantly reducing the labor associated with taking one type of design medium and turning it into another.

While mosaics, brick walls, stained-glass windows, and panelized facades can all be considered tessellated, the term can also refer, in digital design, to approximating surfaces, often singly or doubly curved, with polygonal meshes. Curved surfaces are typically far more complex and expensive to construct than flat ones, and tessellation offers a way to build smooth form using sheet material. This chapter concentrates on how the two—digital surface definition and tessellated construction methodology— are brought together through digital fabrication.

Tessellation, or tiling, is becoming increasingly relevant to building as architects strive to make large, often complex forms and surfaces with standard-size sheet materials. Whereas in modern architecture, tessellation has been the result of using industrialized products such as ceramic tiles, siding, and bricks, it can now be created from nonstandard units. Architects have certainly made intricate patterns from conventional materials such as brick and masonry, but tiling has found new potency in the arena of digital manufacture, which has unique abilities to modulate, design, and build custom panels. Rather than rely on what is commercially available, architects can, using digital-manufacturing techniques, cut pieces from larger stock in multiple differentiated sizes and shapes.

There are two primary ways to model three-dimensional forms digitally: NURBS and meshes. A single project will often be defined in both formats at different stages of the design process. NURBS modelers build smooth curves and surfaces, and they will be discussed at greater length in a later chapter. Mesh modelers use polygons and subdivisions to approximate smooth surfaces. Polygonal meshes, usually made up of triangles and quadrilaterals, are the most widely used; subdivision surfaces use a secondary, more complex algorithm to approximate curvature. Both create additional vertices, edges, and faces that break the surface into tiles. Hence a polygon or subdivided mesh is a tessellated surface.

Depending on the resolution of tessellation, approximated surfaces can be smooth and precise, or faceted and crude. Although it may seem desirable to be highly accurate all the time, this is not necessarily the case. It is often unnecessary to overtessellate a form: it results in a cumbersome and heavy computer model and often in unbuildable form. When evaluating tessellation strategies, if the aim is to calibrate the initial form with a constructional system, one may better determine

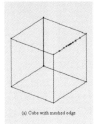

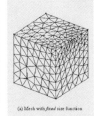
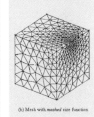

(a) Cube with meshed edge   (b) Mesh without size function   (a) Mesh with *fixed* size function   (b) Mesh with *meshed* size function

the size and resolution of the tiles relative to overall geometry and design intention, and with regard to final building materials and fabrication processes.

Buckminster Fuller's geodesic domes are early examples of such approximation. Fuller's pursuit of lightness and engineered efficiency is epitomized in the domes he designed for mass production and ubiquitous use. Though they did not catch on as he intended, many of his domes were actually built in a variety of tessellated patterns. In every case, the spherical shape is redefined as a pattern of triangles or hexagons that provides structural stability and resists shape deformation. The elegance of the structure is dependent on the uniform curvature of the dome. In the geodesics, every strut, opening, and joint detail is identical. While this uniformity contributes to ready constructability and overall material efficiency, it is unrelenting in terms of form. It is therefore not surprising that neither architects nor the population at large embraced the domes as a panacea for modern building.

The past decade and a half has seen the rapid acceleration of discretization—the digital definition of surface as a coordinated set of discrete parts—as a digital and material practice. Not only is it a logical way to describe and build nonorthogonal forms, it is a method that enables architects to modulate and gradate surface and skin. Peter Macapia of labDORA has suggested that one fascination with such surface systems may be "in part a consequence of the changing nature of how we see architecture no longer as a point or an object in space, but rather as a function, a function of grids, of networks, of gradients."[1] LabDORA's work focuses on leveraging digital techniques such as computational fluid dynamics and finite-element analysis for the geometric and material organization of buildings. This process involves using software that evaluates the mechanical and structural performance of form based on fluid criteria. In doing so, Macapia posits that "the grid has become turbulent, and the geometry dirty."[2] Idealized static systems deform, stretch, and pinch to evolve into geometries reflective of these new constraints. The resulting surface definitions and tiling patterns are visible descriptions of invisible forces and are entirely compelling. Both form finding and material organizations coalesce around architectural performance.

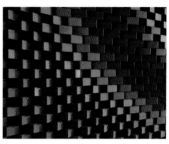

Fabio Gramazio and Matthias Kohler,
Domoterra Lounge, ETH Zürich, 2007.
Plan and elevation; industrial robot
laying brick; completed project.
Photos: Gramazio & Kohler

Macapia's work has methodological ties to the Architectural Association's Emergent Technologies and Design group, led by Michael Weinstock, Achim Menges, and Michael Hensel. Though the group's primary pedagogic concerns are not centered on pattern or tessellation, many of the projects nevertheless examine tiling as the link between overall form finding and material behavior. In his article "Polymorphism," Menges describes the conceptual idea behind the evolution of such architectural systems as akin to natural morphogenesis, as "hierarchical arrangements of relatively simple material components organized through successive series of propagated and differentiated subassemblies from which the system's performative abilities emerge."[3]

This research goes hand in hand with using new and revisited parametric software, such as GenerativeComponents and CATIA. These programs offer the ability to link part to whole with sets of defined geometric relationships. They foster designs wherein a single parametric module takes on multiple variations when instantiated across a field. Even as the design of the field and the module differ, together

they invariably form a tessellated pattern. Software affords a wide array of tessellating possibilities that inevitably propagate certain design techniques, so it is not surprising that there has been a rise in tessellated projects.

On the fabrication end, it appears that this is just the beginning of tessellation possibilities. Fabio Gramazio and Matthias Kohler, both professors at the Swiss Federal Institute of Technology Zurich (more commonly known as the ETH), have made significant strides in revolutionizing computer-aided building in the specific area of assembly and formation of three-dimensional tessellated wall units. Central to this advancement is their adoption of robotics for architectural production. Robots are commonly found in the automotive industry, where they are used to weld, finish, drill, deburr, and handle materials, among other activities. While the strategy of adopting a technology from a more advanced manufacturing industry is the basis of digital fabrication in architecture, the practice in no way undermines Gramazio and Kohler's great leap of imagination. Most striking is how convincingly they have adapted this tool to the

design of sensuous and nonstandard patterned assemblies and formwork.[4]

Unique to robotics is the ability to handle, rotate, drill, and place materials. Robots, like CNC machines, are fed computerized data to direct their work. Not restricted to using subtractive processes such as drilling, however, robots can make subtractive cuts, as well as assemble materials. They can, for example, stack and position building elements, such as bricks or blocks. The robot accurately places the material based on digital data that describes the desired horizontal and vertical placement and orientation. The same data can be used to control drilling operations, as with a vertical five-axis CNC router. The two projects shown here utilize both these techniques and represent just a few of the compelling outcomes of Gramazio and Kohler's teaching research.

The Programmed Wall was one of the team's first robotic investigations. The requisite digital model involved the making and use of a simple brick as an aggregative module. Computer scripts were then written to assemble the modules digitally, addressing the necessary constraints of traditional brick construction, such as coursing and material overlap. The scripts were also written to orient the bricks according to qualities such as porosity and wall profile. Once the design was finalized, data pertaining to size, coursing layer, and the orientation of each brick were given a set of relevant numerical values and exported using proprietary machine software. The robot used this data to assemble the wall brick by brick, much as a traditional mason would have. The result is a fluid and variable gradient field made of identical units.

Like Gramazio and Kohler, SHoP is capitalizing on the sensuous potential of brick tiling, specifically for the creation of large curtain-wall panels. For a site at 290 Mullberry Street in New York City, for example, the firm is proposing a decorative, undulating masonry facade. Though it won't be laid by robots, the pattern is generated using digital scripts. The insulation layer is digitally milled and becomes a positioning template for the brick, which is then grouted into place to form panels. One of the most striking aspects of this and other SHoP projects is the visual and tactile richness achieved through the modulated treatment of highly standard building

Coop Himmelb(l)au, BMW Welt,
Munich, Germany, 2007.
Roof tessellation; "double cone".
Photos: Ari Marcopoulos

materials. This conversation between tile and surface organization is a routine part of designing tessellations; it is by no means mundane, however. Like the previously mentioned work, this project reconsiders and expands on the potential of elevation, surface, and tiling as a design medium.

By contrast, a number of large-scale projects—such as the BMW Welt by Coop Himmelb(l)au, *Acoustic Barrier* by Kas Oosterhuis, and the Smithsonian Institution renovation by Foster & Partners—are an evolution from the mass-produced systems traditionally enabled by digital processes. The ability to array unique panels across large surfaces to address multiple scales and curvatures is one of the great advantages of tessellation. The signature "double cone" of Coop Himmelb(l)au's BMW Welt is a good example of this capability: the basic mesh size of the cone relates fractally to the structural roof grid. The panels are halved, then triangulated to work with the geometry of the cone and the flat glass panes. At a visual and material level, this tiling strategy smoothly synthesizes the dynamic structural surface of the roof and double cone.

Working on a much smaller scale—and with far more limited means—the projects that follow amply describe the design potentials of tessellation, as well as the multiple ways in which digital fabrication is integral to the design dialogue. The work shown here examines the patternistic, visual, structural, and dynamic possibilities of tiled skins. On a practical level, breaking surfaces into smaller pieces that can be easily handled by one or two people is conducive to the kind of design-build experiments explored in

a handful of emerging practices. The *Huyghe + Le Corbusier Puppet Theater* at Harvard's Carpenter Center for the Visual Arts, designed by MOS and built in collaboration with students from the Harvard Graduate School of Design, divides an open volume into diagonal tiles, formed as pans with side flanges to create stiffness and depth. The pans are simply bolted together along adjacent flanges and integrated with small steel ribs for additional spanning support. The project also employs the three-dimensional tile as a structural and planting surface. The pans, filled with moss-covered soil, articulate the seams that define the gradated pattern.

Helios House, designed by Office dA and Johnston Marklee, also highlights seams—half-inch reveals, in this case—to accommodate and accentuate the faceted language of the form. The stainless steel panels themselves are clad over a steel framework and formed substrate. While these substrate panels provide the geometric base on which to attach the cladding tiles, they are much cruder in surface definition, sometimes spanning large, flat areas. The tiles provide a finer grain, visually homogenizing the surface while adding intricacy through the material definition created by subtle changes in reflection, shade, and light. The tessellation pattern, in other words, is the direct result not of the building form (in which case there would be large tiles over flatter areas and smaller ones where demanded by sharp bends) but of remapping the surface to synthesize and equalize its visual affects. Such is the real potential of tessellation.

Foster + Partners, Smithsonian Institution,
Washington, D.C., 2004–7.
Photos: Nigel Young/Foster + Partners

One can generate relatively automatic tiling based simply on geometry, but one can also supersede it.

In *California: Stage Set for John Jasperse* by Ammar Eloueini, the tessellated pattern creates an operable surface structure. It does so by splitting the large, rectangular surface into a field of triangles whose seams are only loosely held together. The triangular tiles are sized to allow not only for great flexibility but also for their neatly lying together during travel. Once assembled, the tiles work together dynamically, sometimes united as a whole operable surface, at other times divided along major seams. Tessellation is made a theatrical device.

The projects included here also simply and eloquently cut and recombine sheet material. *Airspace Tokyo*, by Thom Faulders, celebrates tessellation as pattern yet suppresses it constructionally. The straightforward rectangular panels are welded together to form a seamless screen. The tessellation pattern is, in this case, achieved through cutouts in sheet metal. The openings' size and shape are determined by using a parametric software program to manipulate a tiling pattern based on the Voronoi diagram—a geometric pattern found in nature. Layers of tree leaves were the inspiration, and then the imagery was highly abstracted as overlapping layers of cut aluminum sheets. The result evokes both an interior and an exterior effect of filtered light.

Technicolor Bloom, an installation by Brennan Buck at the University of Applied Arts Vienna, also synthesizes pattern with visual experience. The overall form of the project is a set of smoothly warped surfaces that stretch from one end of the gallery to the other. Each surface is inscribed with a lacelike pattern, generated by a predefined recursive software subdivision algorithm. The densities of the subdivisions (sometimes referred to as "subdivs" or "sub-d's") in part relate the shape of the doubly curved surface but also optically obscure and enhance the larger geometric system. The intricate aperture pattern is formed by a third-degree subdivision (i.e., the surface has been subdivided three times), while the structure is organized along the first; the panels are cut at this larger scale, where structural ribs connect the inner and outer layers. The project thus binds together considerations of constructability, structure, and surface pattern by using the Voronoi system in a self-similar manner for the panels and the cutout texture. This pattern is also nuanced where the inside and outside skins at times take on differentiated porosities, thereby enhancing the illusion of thickness and depth.

A last example, Atelier Manferdini's *West Coast Pavilion*, also utilizes self-similarity to generate its tessellated surface. It is perhaps one of the most comprehensive digital-fabrication projects because it uses a variety of tools to make the layered enclosure. The base structure is a diamond-shaped lattice made of MDF, cut with a CNC router from 2D AutoCAD templates in a process similar to those described earlier in "Sectioning." It is in the filigreed surface, however, that the design intentions are most elaborated. The infill panels comprise fractal tiles—tiles subdivided rather than modulated—so that the tessellation pattern resides locally as well as globally and spans multiple scales.

Like the suppleness of Elena Manferdini's laser-cut clothing, the material property of the pavilion's metal sheets is drawn out by virtue of slicing and letting it take on a three-dimensionality. Making perforations usually requires a cutting technique that drops residual material from the cut holes. Manferdini, however, repositions this manufacturing method and leverages it for surface effect: rather than discard the drops—the small pieces that fall out of the sheet—the metal is reattached to the sheet as a secondary system that casts shadows and catches light. The panels, strung together more like jewelry than building materials, define a new level of intricacy for an architectural skin.

This intricacy permeates much of the work in this chapter, which shows the efforts of a number of architects to cultivate an expanded language of surface subdivision and modulation. In each case, that expanded language is coupled with performance criteria, whether constructional, structural, material, spatial, perceptual, programmatic, or—what is most often the case—a combination thereof. The very synthesis of these concerns, realized through the digital creation and ultimate surface definition of the schemes, is what supports the technological implications of pattern. As these projects demonstrate, the territory of tessellation reaches far and wide.

Photo: Courtesy Atelier Manferdini

West Coast Pavilion
Atelier Manferdini, 2006

The pavilion is a sandwich of undulating layers that diverge and coalesce around and through its volume. The surface of the skin, combined with the diamond-shaped structure, behaves like three-dimensional lacework, creating a dynamic screening and filtering effect.

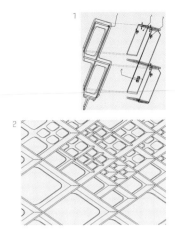

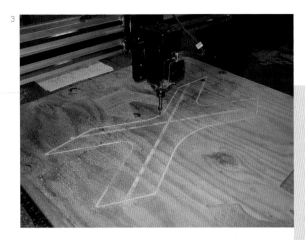

Atelier Manferdini, *West Coast Pavilion*, Architectural Biennial Beijing, 2006.
All photos: Courtesy Atelier Manferdini (except where indicated)

1 Construction diagram of plywood structure, ribs, and facing.
2 Diagram of tessellation subdivision.
3 CNC-routing plywood for inner structure.
4 Assembled wall, from exterior. Photo: Courtesy Neil Leach.
5 Assembled plywood and MDF wall structure. Photo: Courtesy Neil Leach.
6 Laser-cutting metal cladding panel. Photo: Courtesy Jae Rodriguez.
7 Templates for laser-cutting metal cladding panels.
8 Cut, folded, and assembled metal cladding panels. Photo: Courtesy Neil Leach

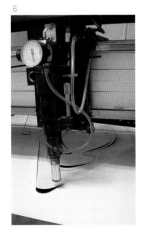

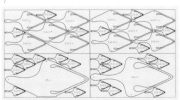

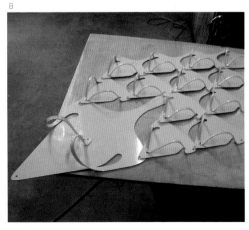

LEFT: Atelier Manferdini, *Cherry Blossom Collection*,
Spring-Summer 2007. Photo: Robert Robert
BELOW AND OPPOSITE: **Completed project.**
Photos: Courtesy Atelier Manferdini

Photo: Florian Holzherr

Huyghe + Le Corbusier Puppet Theater
MOS, 2004

To celebrate the fortieth anniversary of Le Corbusier's Carpenter Center for the Visual Arts at Harvard University—his only North American project—this theater was constructed within the site's sunken exterior courtyard specifically for a puppet performance by the conceptual artist Pierre Huyghe. The organic form of the theater was built with five hundred unique white polycarbonate panels, diamond-shaped and interlocking to create a rigid structure; because they are simply bolted together, they are easily assembled and disassembled. Forces dissipate across the assembled surface, which encloses the theater space, and the modulated ceiling panels are turned inside out to create skylights and, like keystones, structural stability. The panels are three inches in depth and span more than fifteen feet at the center of the theater. Foam inserts placed in the panels stiffen the plastic shell. An exterior layer of moss covers the plastic panels, so at night, when light permeates the edges of the diagonal plastic panels, the moss appears suspended.

Entering the theater from Quincy Street through a soft, flexible opening focused around a tree, the space bulges to form an interior of reflective, glossy, white plastic walls. Undulating white foam seating repeats the patterning and dimension of the plastic panels, creating a uniform vessel. The interior compresses, looking toward the stage opening. When the puppet performance isn't playing, there is a view into the Carpenter Center, while the soft entrance frames a single tree as one exits. The theater collapses the synthetic and organic into a single structural surface.

LEFT: **Moss-filled panel.** Photo: Michael Vahrenwald
BELOW: **Assembly.** Photo: MOS

ABOVE: **Interior view.** Photo: Michael Vahrenwald
BELOW: **CATIA model.** Photo: MOS

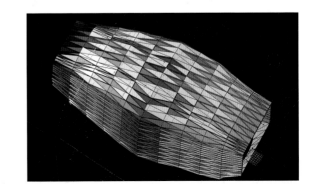

All photos: Eric Staudenmaier

Helios House
Office dA and Johnston Marklee & Associates, 2006–7

The design of *Helios House* embraces the paradox of creating a green gas station. Conceived as a learning lab, *Helios House* was designed to stimulate dialogue, promote education, and foster discussion on the topic of environmental stewardship. The water, heat, energy, lighting, and material systems of *Helios House* were all built to maximize sustainability and energy efficiency, and the canopy design is the house's most emblematic feature.

This project develops a unique formal logic to integrate the gas station's functions into a seamless whole. The surface works as a parametric tessellation to incorporate various architectural and technical features. Thus the pay kiosk, the structure, the sign panels, and the canopy are all shaped from the same faceted surface. The triangulated stainless-steel panels reconcile complex and sometimes contradictory requirements of the site, program, codes, and zoning ordinances, while they establish the site identity and core of the brand experience. They are also responsible for the unique profile of the canopy and offer an alternative branding strategy to the typical gas-station composition, which conceptualizes the canopy simply as an armature for the logo. Throughout the project, the fabrication and design systems were optimized to conserve labor costs and reduce material waste. The canopy, which was developed with a design/build fabricator, incorporates 1,653 stainless-steel panels into a prefabricated assembly system. Fastened together off-site, the canopy comprises fifty-two transportable components, which were then erected on-site in just four weeks. The efficiency and precision of this technique taps the potential of mass customization by using the controlled environment of a shop to calibrate modular components, each having unique geometric conditions.

ABOVE, CLOCKWISE FROM TOP LEFT: Formed substrate panel; prefabricated substrate panels; on-site construction; on-site construction; stainless steel cladding on prefabricated substrate; on-site construction.
BELOW: Completed project.

California: Stage Set for John Jasperse
AEDS/Ammar Eloueini, 2003

California is a dance piece developed by the choreographer John Jasperse and performed by his company. As opposed to serving as a backdrop of immobile form for the stage, the set was designed as a morphing structure that allowed the dancers to engage directly with the architectural piece.

The design is modeled from a computer-generated surface, the form of which was developed to allow for maximum flexibility, creating a geometrically and spatially changing set that emulates and adapts to the performers' movements. Using a basic fabric-pattern layout, the design unfolded into individual segments that piece together to form the transformable surface. The primary material is polycarbonate, maintaining translucency and reflectivity so the surface absorbs and diffuses light. Zip ties secure the segments and allow for flexibility and ease of construction. The set can be created in hours and is easily broken down and packed into boxes to be reconstructed elsewhere.

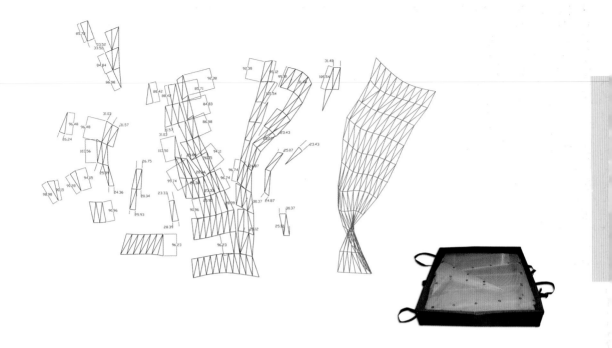

ABOVE LEFT: Surface unfolded flat into panels.
ABOVE RIGHT: Four-by-four traveling case.
OPPOSITE AND BELOW: Stage set in operation.

 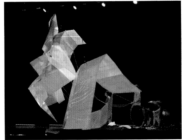

Photo: Thom Faulders Architecture

Airspace Tokyo
Thom Faulders Architecture, 2007

This project creates an exterior building skin for a new four-story multifamily dwelling with photography studios in Tokyo, Japan. Located in the Kita-Magome Ota-ku district, the site was previously occupied by the owner's family, in a residence uniquely wrapped by a layer of dense vegetation. To accommodate the construction of the new, larger development, the entire site is designated to be razed, so the *Airspace* design embodies an architectural system that performs with attributes similar to the demolished green strip and creates an atmospheric space of activity.

Conceived as a thin interstitial environment, the articulated densities of the new open-celled meshwork are layered in response to the inner workings of the building's program. *Airspace* is a zone where the artificial blends with nature: sunlight is refracted along its metallic surfaces; rainwater is channeled away from exterior walkways via capillary action; and interior views are shielded by its variegated and foliage-like cover.

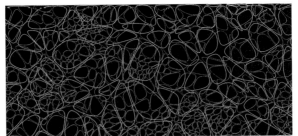

LEFT: **Double-skin overlay.** Photo: Thom Faulders Architecture
RIGHT: **Tree-canopy inspiration.** Photo: Thom Faulders Architecture
BELOW: **Diagram of structural lines for panels.**
BOTTOM: **Completed screen.** Photo: Studio M

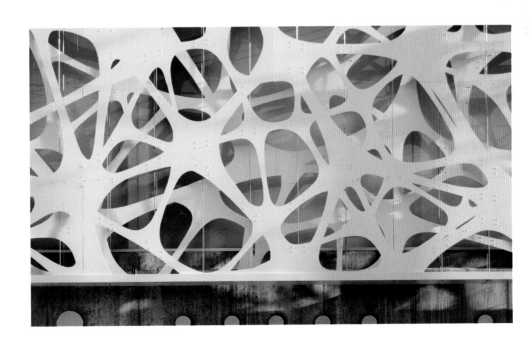

Photo: Christof Gaggl

Technicolor Bloom
Brennan Buck, 2007

Technicolor Bloom is a full-scale prototype that produces doubly curved, digitally designed geometry, using completely standard, scalable fabrication technology. It proposes a method and a set of aesthetic principles that extend the architectural potential of topological form by incorporating such architectural systems as structure, aperture, fenestration, and construction directly into the project's geometry. Built from fourteen hundred uniquely cut, flat plywood panels, the installation favors intense detail over seamless elegance. At the same time, it proliferates continuity: continuity of surface morphology, continuity of the structural patterns across those surfaces, and varied interrelationships of depth and color from one surface to the next. The result is a kaleidoscopic study of the literal and phenomenal effects of three-dimensional pattern. These patterns reinforce the geometry they define in one moment and cloud it the next. Finally, the installation proposes a variation of architectural figure that evokes loose, variable associations while remaining in the realm of affect.

Technologically, the project is comparable to the Technicolor film process, which multiplies the visual intensity of film through the superimposition of three primary colors. *Technicolor Bloom* embraces the geometry of subdivision surfaces and techniques of computation but treats them as a given rather than as motivation. While adaptive tessellation algorithms were used to produce the initial patterns, parametric design, with its associated discourses of efficiency and automated authorship, was suppressed in favor of specific design intention and the precise control of visual effects. In addition to pattern variations, a series of techniques were used to multiply the affective qualities of the patterned surface. Surfaces were layered at various depths to produce moirés and other effects, while individual structural members were thickened or trimmed down to emphasize a network of figures that materialize and fade away within the overall pattern.

ABOVE: Laser-cut panels, test mock-up, installation.
BELOW: Panel-cutting templates.
BOTTOM: Details showing converging pattern.
Photos: Brennan Buck

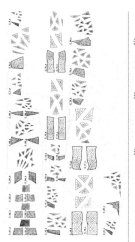
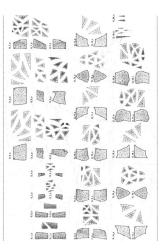
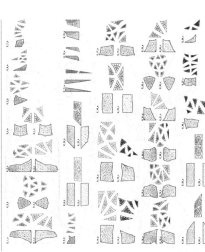

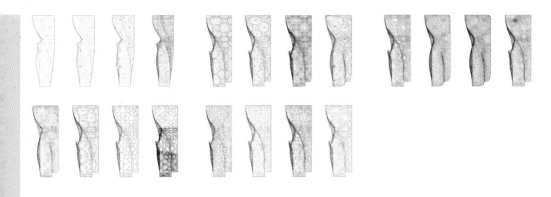

ABOVE: **Tessellation studies.** Photo: Brennan Buck
BELOW: View from above.
OPPOSITE: View from inside.
Photos below and opposite: Christof Gaggl

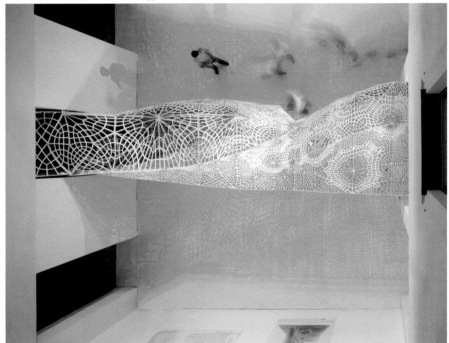

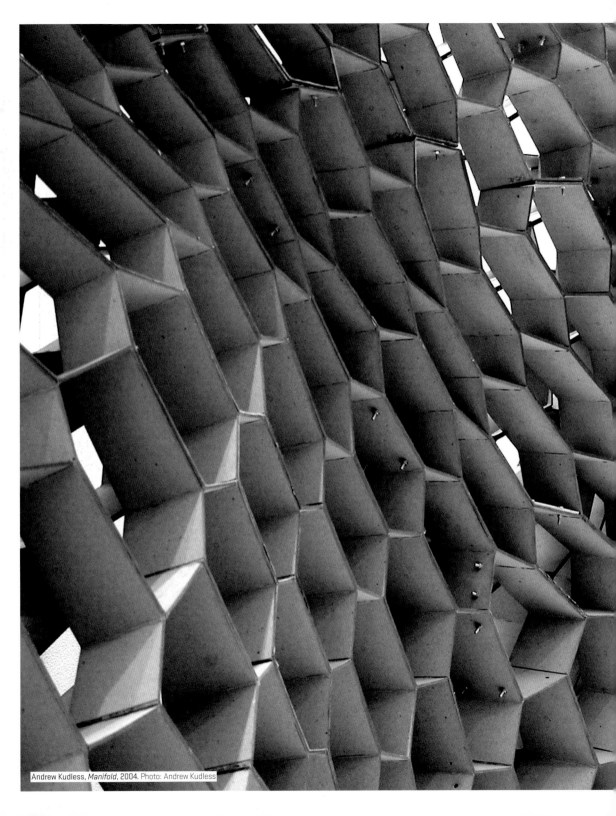
Andrew Kudless, *Manifold*, 2004. Photo: Andrew Kudless

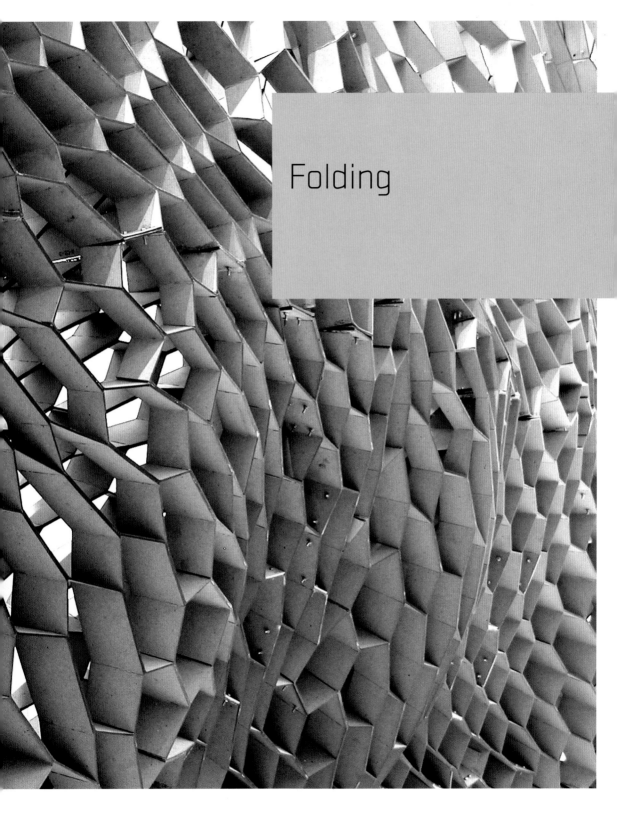

Folding

Folding turns a flat surface into a three-dimensional one. It is a powerful technique not only for making form but also for creating structure with geometry. When folds are introduced into otherwise planar materials, those materials gain stiffness and rigidity, can span distance, and can often be self-supporting. Folding is materially economical, visually appealing, and effective at multiple scales. It is not surprising that architects have expanded its use in the digital age.

In architecture, folding is theoretical concept, formal tactic, and the most literally material operation. Naturally, this chapter focuses on the material operation, but it is helpful to speak about it in the context of its other associations. In all cases, folding, or pleating, allows new spaces and territories to emerge without losing the native characteristics of what is being folded. It is already well understood that an architectural aspiration for the fold lies in its potential for manifesting cohesion and a continuity of competing spatial, cultural, social, programmatic, and contextual conditions within a single language. Greg Lynn argued in 1993 that "if there is a single effect produced in the architecture of folding, it will be the ability to integrate unrelated elements within a new continuous mixture."[1]

For roughly the past fifteen years, architects have certainly embraced the technique and progressively created continuous surfaces, spaces, and forms. Critics have rightly argued that the mere physicalization of the fold can in no way approach the complexities embedded in the concept; the fold, like all other theoretical and conceptual constructs, necessarily exceeds the formal domain of architecture. It has nevertheless produced a range of compelling work that has undeniably shaped contemporary design. Within this language, the actual folding of material is in part the simple and direct result of the process of producing a building in line with its conceptual aspirations. If floors fold to become walls and ceilings, then the material must fold as well. The examples are extensive and wide-ranging. The curved plywood walls of the Office for Metropolitan Architecture's *Educatorium*, the wrapped metal corner panels of Daniel Libeskind's Jewish Museum Berlin, and the structural cladding of Foreign Office Architects' Yokohama International Port Terminal are all instances of making the material perform in a manner consistent with the overall architecture.

As a material technique, however, folding is not limited to being a secondary system of articulating the larger building diagram. The operation of folding material is also a generative design tool that has gained currency in digital-fabrication processes. Like folding as a conceptual architectural device, it shares the aspiration to create fluidity and multifunctionality with continuous surface. Folding expands the three-dimensional vocabulary of surface by naturally producing deformation and inflection. Digital tools enable subtle and complex geometric modulations, affording the ability to both incorporate and smooth over difference. The structural stiffness produced by introducing folds into material is another significant advantage of the technique.

It is worth noting the design precedents that examined the structural potential of folding. The early and mid-twentieth century was an era of structural and architectural experimentation, fueled by engineers such as Félix Candela, Eduardo Catalano, Pier Luigi Nervi, and Eduardo Torroja. These engineer-architects strove for structural elegance and material lightness in the shaping of thin-shell concrete buildings. The projects were frequently designed around creased forms and hyperbolic curvature to create roof structures. Folded plate structures, a simpler geometric model, were also prevalent at the time. Whereas the hypar surfaces were somewhat rarified, accordion-shaped concrete roofs became quite common in many parts of the world. The relative ease of making the formwork, along with the structural potential of casting concrete into a folded form, made an efficient and popular combination. Yet, economy aside, these buildings were a new generation of architecture that used geometry to couple structural performance and enclosure.

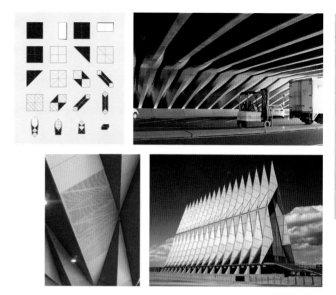

A project that modifies normative reinforced-concrete structural profiles to a folded aesthetic is the underside service zone of the Sydney Opera House. A far less celebrated aspect of Jørn Utzon's masterwork, this zone is a set of undulating beams made of formed, folded concrete. What is ordinarily a hierarchical configuration of rectangular beams supporting a flat slab is transformed here into a structural ceiling landscape. In other cases, folding is the conceptual as well as the tectonic driver. The Air Force Academy Cadet Chapel, by Walter Netsch and Skidmore, Owings & Merrill, completed in 1962, merges roof and wall using prismatic folds. Smaller-scale examples also sprang from prismatic folding exercises. Heinrich Engel's book *Structure Systems* uses scaled paper models to illustrate folded-plate, two- and three-hinge frames, cross-folded surfaces, and a variety of other inventive folded structures.[2] These were often not built to full scale, but the models stimulated a range of work caught in the productive realm between architecture and industrial design.

Of course, folding is not limited to structural tectonics. Representing a method that transforms two dimensions into three, these projects describe its rich potential to make surface itself a modulated three-dimensional spatial construct. Folding has a long history in craft-based practices and product design, and it is in this context that digital tools are bridging a traditionally object-oriented practice and architecturally scaled work. With digital fabrication, folding takes on a new dimension and is extended to a method of making: building materials are literally folded into place. Of all the techniques described in this book, folding offers perhaps the greatest potential for variety because it is inherently capable of manifesting a wide range of forms. Creased surfaces, folded plates, and wrapped volumes all fall within the purview of folding. These building methods share a similar fabrication process (three-dimensional surfaces are developed—that is, unrolled or unfolded) to make two-dimensional templates for cutting.

As it has for other digital methods, software has enabled and streamlined the translation from three dimensions to two. Modeling programs such as Rhinoceros have embedded commands that efficiently unroll singly curved surfaces. There is also a group of commercially available programs

FROM LEFT:

Office dA, *Fabricating Coincidences*,
Museum of Modern Art, New York, 1998.
Photo: Dan Bibb

Haresh Lalvani/AlgoRhythm Technologies,
InterRipples Ceiling System.
Photo: Robert Wrazen; prototype: Milgo-Bufkin,
courtesy Haresh Lalvani

and plug-ins (e.g., Lamina Design, Surf Master, and Pepakura Designer), as well as sheet-metal and other engineering software (SolidWorks and LITIO), that is specifically designed to turn free-form surfaces into a collection of flat pieces. These programs take material thickness into account and often offer options for jointing and labeling. The range of software available is an indication of how prevalent folding is as a material technique. Most of it is aimed at the craft, industrial-design, and sheet-metal industries, but it is equally applicable to architecture.

On the machine side, laser cutters are frequently used to make materials foldable. Unlike other three-axis machines, lasers are designed for engraving and can easily execute different line types, such as dashed, dotted, and scored. They can therefore make seams in a variety of methods without sacrificing the integrity of the material. Water-jet and plasma cutters are also widely used. These are aimed at cutting metals and do not have the ability to score, but they can readily make other types of perforations to control where the material creases.

As for material selection, because it must be restricted to those that are pliable and capable of bending without breaking, the materials that other industries commonly use to fold up parts—sheet metal, thick paper, and fabric—are also frequently called on by architects. Early executions of digitally fabricated folded surfaces simultaneously relied on standard sheet-metal practices and extended the aesthetic and formal possibilities of the material using digital techniques. Two good examples of these early efforts are Office dA's installation, *Fabricating*

Coincidences, for MoMA's "Fabrications" exhibition in 1998 and Haresh Lalvani's sinuous metal panels and column covers for AlgoRhythm Technologies.

Although the initial design of *Fabricating Coincidences* was largely done by hand, its manufacture relied heavily on both computerized punching and laser cutting. Of particular note is the seam detail, which the architects redesigned as a "stitch." This seam is made by overlapping dashed laser cuts to minimize material at the bend and make crisp and continuous folds. Unlike typical sheet-metal bending, which uses a break and results in radiused corners, this new method takes advantage of the digital process both to cut and to perforate the panels and to obtain crisp edges. The project uses these types of folds exclusively, not only for aesthetic effect but also to unite surface and structure. The tight seams allow for the rear supports to multiply in thickness and essentially to stack as both columns and footings.

Seams are also at the cornerstone of Haresh Lalvani's research for AlgoRhythm Technologies. In his case, though, it is the geometry that departs from standard practice. Folds take on hyperbolic shapes generated by mathematical algorithms, and the seams guide the sinuous bends. These curved creases provide structural stability while dramatically redefining the sheet metal as sets of alternating convex and concave surfaces. The curved seams and internal stresses hold the dished shapes smooth. Particularly exciting is that the effectiveness of this technique depends on the elastic and plastic properties of the material, thus requiring a close affiliation between material and fabrication method.

Unlike sectioning, for example, a technique that is somewhat irrespective of material in that material properties do not inherently change when cut in section, folding relies on the characteristics of the original material as it adds a new visual, spatial, and tectonic dimension.

This aspect of folding holds true at a large scale, too, where the design of the building skin has become a preoccupation of many contemporary architects. In *The Function of Ornament*, Farshid Moussavi and Michael Kubo attribute the current architectural transition toward ornament and building enclosure to affect and its sensorial and abstract communicative potential.[3] Whether this potential accounts for the fundamental shift in attention toward surface and skin, there is no doubt that there is a current obsession for work that produces material and atmospheric effect, sometimes together with functional criteria. For example, the Walker Art Center Expansion by Herzog & de Meuron, which has long been fascinated with the essential characteristics of material and its associative potential, uses a light creasing operation to create the crinkled facade. Folding is here generated largely for patternistic and ornamental purposes: the building shimmers. However, folding also serves the purpose of eliminating unanticipated oil-canning in favor of a precisely disturbed facade. Like all digital-fabrication practices, this folded skin has precedents in conventional construction. In the case of the Walker Art Center Expansion, flat-seam metal shingles and standing seam panels are standardized precursors. Yet, again, what is distinct about this new crop of work is how architects have adapted traditional methods to use folding as an operational system that manifests diversity in a highly specific and constructed manner. The projects in this chapter use such folded systems to make surface, volume, and structure.

Surface projects include *Nubik* by AEDS/Ammar Eloueini and *In-Out Curtain* by IwamotoScott: both develop a system of cuts and folds for a series of self-similar pieces that combine to create a modulated surface. *Nubik* is one of a series of projects by Ammar Eloueini that investigate the luminous, flexible, sculptural potential of pleated translucent polycarbonate. While the majority of Eloueini's work consists of fabriclike surfaces made of triangulated tessellations, this project comprises snaking linear strands. Each expresses a subtly changing rhythm of bulging "pods" and flat connectors built of the same material. The resulting aggregation locks together rigidly in a glowing cloudlike array.

IwamotoScott's *In-Out Curtain* also works to deflect direct light while it aims for a flexible end product. The design takes principles from modular origami—using folds and creases, for example, to make modules that interlock to form a collective whole—while simple material resistance generates its transformable quality. Each module is designed so that it holds two distinct shapes: in and out, which correspond to a closed/concave shape and an open/convex one. When torqued, the modules translate their individual deformations onto adjacent areas, creating a curtain of multiple shape variations. Folding, in this case, becomes a dynamic system, as well as a method of making.

While these two projects work with thickness and depth, they essentially remain surfaces. Other projects focus more specifically on achieving volume through folding. Like cardboard boxes, paper bags, and a host of other common products, folding has repeatedly proven an effective and elegant method for making three-dimensional form. The folds provide rigidity without requiring a lot of material to contain substantial areas of empty space. In other words, weight to volume, folds are highly efficient. The following projects are concerned with making volume and include Chris Bosse's *Entry Paradise Pavilion* and Hitoshi Abe's Aoba-tei restaurant. These two projects adapt parallel practices from clothing manufacturing. Folds here are soft and rely on the flexibility of the fabric or sheet metal to generate volume. Like clothes, they display the effects of draping, stretching, and seaming to arrive at the final form. Particular to both projects is the necessity of aligning material choice with the desired effect.

Chris Bosse's *Entry Paradise Pavilion*, designed for an exhibition in Germany in 2006, is based on similar soap-bubble geometry, but it capitalizes on the tensile properties of lightweight Lycra fabric. Similarly to *Loop*, the design physicalizes the lines and surface tension of soap films. These seams are made tubular and expanded to form a continuous tensile framework. Bosse's pavilion, however, stands in significant contrast to *Loop*, which relies on the warped shape of the rings to introduce internal pressures and create compressive forces among adjacent cells, thereby increasing the overall structural capacity of the cellular network. The design of the *Entry Paradise Pavilion*, on the other hand, takes cues from minimal surface tent structures and expands the volumetric potential of this construction technique. Bosse used specialized sail-making software to refine the surface geometries and equalize the internal tensions of the material. The result is a taut surface, held in tension at points on the ceiling and floor. *Entry Paradise Pavilion* captures space by stitching together a pliable material into smooth yet ultimately still-folded surfaces.

The soft bend also defines the interior liner of Hitoshi Abe's Aoba-tei restaurant, which combines folding with other advanced fabrication processes—forming and perforating. The 2.3-millimeter-thick steel liner was conceived as a flat sheet folded into the space using conically curved corners. The construction process used digital shipbuilding technology to unfold this three-dimensional form into two-dimensional plates, taking into consideration the thickness and ductile properties of the material. Shipbuilders experienced in working with steel plate also assembled, formed, and welded the steel plates together. While the essence of the project relies on folding as the primary digital operation, steel clearly cannot be easily folded into place on-site. Instead, the construction team formed the steel by heating and cooling it along relevant seams.

Perforation is another automated fabrication technique, and its use here not only advances digital-fabrication processes but also pursues a powerful design thread in its abstraction and rerepresentation of elements in nature through simulated architectural affects. For this wholly interior project, dappling is made atmospheric using tree canopies as the visual metaphor. Before being bent, each panel was first perforated by a CNC turret with three differently sized holes on a fifteen-millimeter grid. This perforated liner forms a deep forestlike experience whereby the primary light source is thousands of pinpoints of light.

Lastly, contemporary architects, like their predecessors, have leapt on one of the great advantages of folding, which is its ability to provide structure. While the above-mentioned examples describe structures made through folded forms, a crop of new work is investigating material folding as a structural technique. Particularly compelling is the scaled-down, distributed model of structure that emerges out of material size. The following projects explore structural surface and the consequent visual and material implications: *Digital Origami* by Chris Bosse, *C_Wall* and *Manifold* by Andrew Kudless, and *Dragonfly* by EMERGENT'S Tom Wiscombe.

Digital Origami and *C_Wall* both transform sheet material into structural building blocks. Both laser-cut and engrave and fold paper to make stackable modules. The designs differ significantly, however, in conception and result. As the designer, for PTW Architects, of the National Aquatics Center for the 2008 Olympics in Beijing, Bosse takes efficiencies employed in the structural envelope of the building to limit the number of cells while maximizing visual difference. Also known as the *Watercube*, the design employs a cellular organization based on foam, or the Weaire-Phelan structure, reputedly the most efficient cellular partitioning arrangement. It is composed of two types of irregular polyhedra—six tetrakaidecahedra (fourteen-sided) and two dodecahedra (twelve-sided)—that nest together to form a larger interlocking unit. Yet whereas the *Watercube* shears a large block of packed cells to arrive at the final interior and exterior surfaces, *Digital Origami* allows

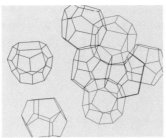

its thirty-five hundred recycled cardboard units to aggregate organically. The simplicity of the project's construction method is belied by its visual complexity. The bottom-up structural logic fosters on-site design flexibility. Cells are left out at times for porosity, the outside fringes of the installation suggest possible future growth, and the design can be infinitely reconfigured to respond to different site conditions and constraints.

The cellular units of Andrew Kudless's *C_Wall*, by contrast, are designed to fill a predetermined volume: one wythe thick. The Voronoi cells are generated using a computer script that uses points projected on the faceted surfaces of the form. Unlike the regularized eight modules of *Digital Origami*, each cell shape of *C_Wall* is unique, configured for one specific arrangement: the modular difference gives integrity to the whole. Though intricate and diverse, the units are subsumed into the larger figure of the piece. It is at once organic and constructed.

It is worth noting that *Digital Origami* and *C_Wall* outline two fundamentally different design processes: bottom-up and top-down, respectively. Both installations are laser-cut, made by unfolding and refolding building blocks, and both create distributed structure from a collection of units. The hierarchy in each of module to whole is reversed, however. Digital processes have facilitated the design of such modulated systems. Scripting, in particular, has opened the door to evolutionary design techniques that explore growth patterns and the relationships of part to whole. It is beyond the scope of this book to delve into emergent, evolutionary,

morphogenetic, or biomimetic processes, but it is relevant that the type and scale of each of these projects is a valuable testing ground for this type of research.[4]

The last two projects to be discussed in this chapter, *Manifold* and *Dragonfly*, seek to synthesize the relationship of cellular configuration to overall form. As the previously described projects do, both begin by drawing from systems found in nature. *Manifold* employs a honeycomb structure, while *Dragonfly* draws from the structure of a dragonfly's wing. Rather than use pure geometric units or develop a partitioned infill, these projects work between part and whole. They are in some measure self-organizing, but both internal system and overall formation adjust to each other. Architects have turned to natural systems, as to structural models, as a way to describe this negotiation.

The honeycomb pattern of *Manifold* modulates according to specified performance criteria. Andrew Kudless developed a RhinoScript to deform the pure hexagonal geometry based on alignments and deviations of the front and back walls. The skewed hexagons maintain their topological integrity yet take on an internal dynamic governed by visual density, bearing capacity, and constructional seams in the wall structure.

Finally, EMERGENT's installation, *Dragonfly*, developed in collaboration with the engineering firm Buro Happold for the SCI-Arc Gallery in 2007, investigates the extreme structural and formal properties of the dragonfly wing. EMERGENT'S principal, Tom Wiscombe, states: "In nature, the dragonfly wing is unmatched in its structural performance and exquisite formal variation. Its morphology cannot be traced to any single bio-mathematical minima or optimum, but is rather the complex result of multiple patterning systems interweaving in response to various force flows and material properties."[5] The design process iteratively generated structural mutations based on support conditions for the extreme cantilever while using boundary conditions to interrelate overall form, cell shape, and band depth. Yet, like all good architecture, the project is not a mere reflection of structural determinism. *Dragonfly* evolved simultaneously toward structural performance and visual variation.

To achieve the cantilevered condition, EMERGENT and Buro Happold employed digital optimization routines to refine the structure, as well as to create formal variation in response to local conditions. This effort was linked to a fully parametrized fabrication process. Rather than follow the typical linear, and often laborious, progression from three-dimensional computer model to two-dimensional CAD template, the two were linked together in the modeling environment. Each member was accurately described, including material thickness, scored seams, and bolt holes, in CATIA. They were also digitally labeled with pertinent information, such as location and bending angle. The bands were then automatically unfolded as the computer model evolved structurally and formally. On final iteration, these templates were arranged with RhinoNest (a nesting program that maximizes material usage) on a four-by-eight-foot aluminum sheet and then cut using a CNC router.

As with all construction processes, realizing built form is an imprecise exercise. Digital fabrication, though highly accurate, still falls sway to material fluctuations, fabrication limitations, and other physical constraints. Building *Dragonfly* was no exception. Slight deviation in bending the angles and folds, as well as in the expansion and contraction of the aluminum, naturally created unanticipated consequences. These were dealt with in a manner consistent with both the precision of the digital model and the ductility of the material: the bands were coerced into place with the knowledge that the bolt holes were perfectly aligned. Once suspended, the final cantilevered formation acted as a single cohesive unit, a clear testament to the integrated architectural and engineering design approach.

Dragonfly uses folding for structural performance and lateral connectivity, employing the depth of the bands to span. As with all the projects mentioned in this chapter, folding is treated as an operative language that emanates throughout the schemes formally and functionally. Particular to this technique is its close affiliation to material behavior. Though limiting, it is perhaps this material constraint that makes folding so effective constructionally: it demands that design take the physical world into account from the start.

All photos: Tom Wiscombe/EMERGENT

Dragonfly
Tom Wiscombe/EMERGENT, 2007

In this installation, dragonfly morphology and syntax are employed biomimetically, that is, in terms of formal and behavioral logics rather than pure aesthetics. Dragonfly wings are generated by evolutionary processes involving aerodynamics, lightness, mechanical properties, composite performance, the smooth accumulation of organic material, and the active flow of dragonfly blood. They consist of both honeycomb patterns, which are flexible and exhibit membrane behavior, and ladder-type patterns, which are stiff and exhibit beamlike behavior. *Dragonfly* is governed by a different set of parameters, including gravity and seismic loads, specific support locations and the quality of those supports, flat material increments, and buckling failure—differences that lead to an unpredictable hybrid morphology.

Dragonfly is a cooperative effort of EMERGENT and the innovative engineering firm Buro Happold. It is an experiment in the fluid feedback of design sensibility, engineering innovation, and fabrication logic in a contemporary digital environment wherein these disciplines become enmeshed like never before. This process redefines engineering—which is often about idealized problem solving and formal economy—as a messy evolutionary process closer to speciation in nature. Using boundary conditions relating to overall structural shape, individual cell morphology, vein distribution and pleating, depth, and incremental material thickness, the geometry was evolved simultaneously toward performance and wild variation.

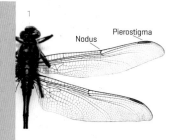

1

Nodus
Pierostigma

2

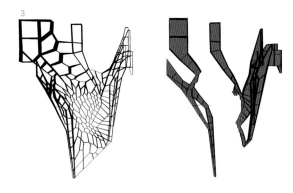

3

1 Dragonfly-wing structure.
2 Structural grid morphologies.
3 Final plan with projected continuous structural ribs.
4 Deformation analysis.
5 CATIA model.
6 Structural stress analysis.
7 Drawing of layered plates showing connection locations.

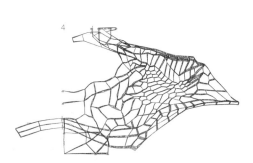

4

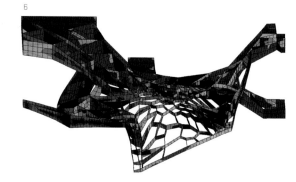

6

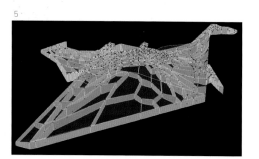

5

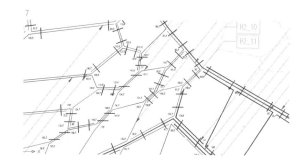

7

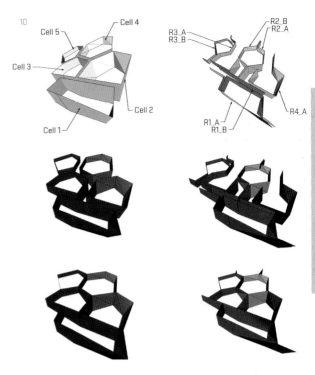

Cell 5
Cell 4
Cell 3
Cell 1
Cell 2

R3_A
R3_B
R2_B
R2_A
R1_A
R1_B
R4_A

8 Laser-cut model.
9 CNC-routed ribs from aluminum plate for mock-up.
10 Digital model of test piece for mock-up.
11 Mock-up.
12 Assembly.

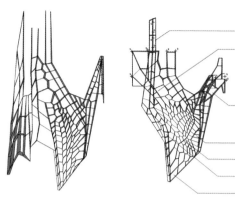

Vein aligns with existing steel of mezzanine and organizes into quad cells for stiffness.

Vein extends out of the honeycomb and connects to existing catwalk for stability.

Arm delaminates and pleats to connect to existing column and create beam action.

Vein splits and hybridizes with honeycomb in response to indeterminate condition.

Vein emerges to create continuity through honeycomb.

Vein emerges and pleats consolidating large loose cells into stiff beam.

Cells at end of cantilever begin to thin out to reduce material weight.

ABOVE: Plan view of structural morphology.
BELOW: Completed installation from above.
OPPOSITE ABOVE: Completed installation from below.
OPPOSITE BELOW: Plan.

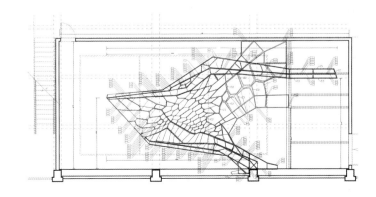

All photos: AEDS/Ammar Eloueini

Nubik
AEDS/Ammar Eloueini, 2005

Nubik was a site-specific installation for the "Mash-Up!" exhibit at Grand Arts gallery in Kansas City, Missouri, in 2005. A series of eight folded strands were suspended from the ceiling by cables. These strands were made out of variously sized pods, so they all share similar roots but are different in their final design. The strands are under the existing skylights to help diffuse the direct sunlight. *Nubik* is designed to keep the existing subdivisions in the space operable, allowing the gallery's spaces to function under various curatorial conditions. It is made out of a translucent, glossy polycarbonate that is very lightweight and has good structural integrity. The panels are attached simply with zip ties to allow maximum flexibility for future mounting and dismounting, as well as for access and adjustments to the space above and below.

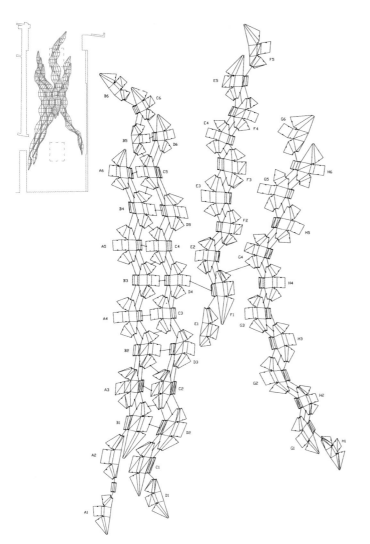

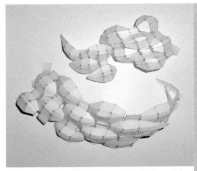

ABOVE: Study model.
LEFT: Unfolded plan of folded surfaces.
BELOW: Assembly and installation.

In-Out Curtain
IwamotoScott, 2005

In-Out Curtain is a prototype design for an operable screen that combines ideas from origami and digital production, focusing in particular on creating a flexible and user-responsive system. Conceived as hybrid drape and Venetian blind, *In-Out Curtain* operates at both the overall and the modular levels and can change shape in section, as well as in plan. It is designed to function as a transformable room partition, enclosure screen, or window shade, whose form can be altered by hand to address movement, interaction, and light.

The modules that make up the curtain are designed so that they hold two distinct shapes: in and out. Both positions rely on internal tensions to maintain their place, and both have a degree of elasticity to allow for switching between positions. When linked together, the modules translate their individual deformations onto adjacent areas, creating a curtain of multiple shape variation.

The overall pattern is easily altered for each application, which means the curtain can not only be designed in its overall dimensions for a particular space but also be systemically responsive in terms of its internal deformations. In the end, the project attains a flexible design and manufacturing system whereby the geometries for the unfolded, flattened module templates are calculated and differentiated using sets of simple, proportional commands.

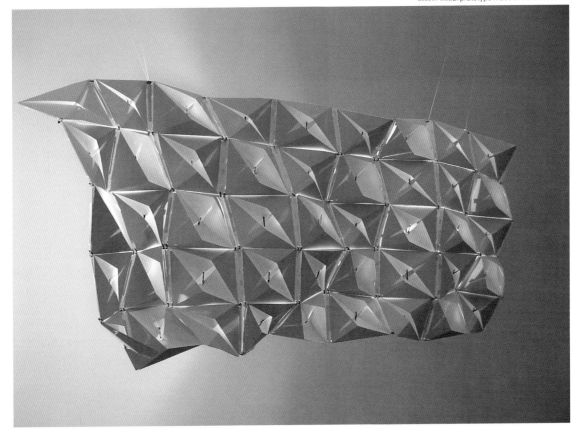

All photos: Chris Bosse

Entry Paradise Pavilion
Chris Bosse/PTW Architects, 2006

Microscopic cell structures were the inspiration for the design of this pavilion that recalls the irregular natural forms of foam, sponge, or coral reefs. Chris Bosse of PTW Architects created these biomorphic shapes using architecture software. The phenomenology and structure of microorganisms like coral polyps or radiolarians are the basis of this computer simulation of naturally evolving systems. The shape of the pavilion is not explicitly designed; it is rather the result of the most efficient subdivisions of three-dimensional space found in nature, those of organic cells, mineral crystals, and the natural formation of soap bubbles. The concept was achieved with a flexible material that follows, as a spiderweb, the forces of gravity, tension, and growth.

The project renounces the application of a structure in the traditional sense. Instead, the space is filled with a three-dimensional lightweight sculpture that is solely based on minimal surface tension, freely stretching between wall, ceiling, and floor. While it appears solid, the structure is actually soft and flexible and creates highly unusual spaces that come to life with projection and lighting.

The project also employed a new digital workflow, enabling the generation of space out of a lightweight material in an extremely short amount of time. The computer model, which was based on the simulation of complexity in naturally evolving systems, feeds directly into a production line of sail-making software and digital manufacturing. The pavilion, weighing only seventeen kilograms, can be transported in a small carry-on bag to any place in the world, can be assembled in less than an hour, and is fully reusable.

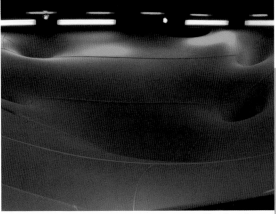

TOP: Views from above.
CENTER: Unrolled panels for CNC cutting
and digital model of minimal surface.
BOTTOM: Project packaged for shipping to Germany.

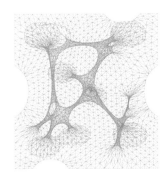

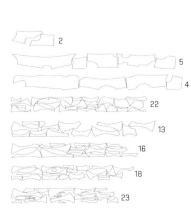

2

5

4

22

13

16

18

23

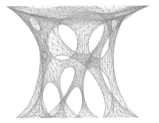

All photos: DAICI ANO/FWD.INC.

Aoba-tei
Atelier Hitoshi Abe, 2004

By inserting a wall of thin steel plates within the interior of a French restaurant in Sendai, Japan, Hitoshi Abe created for this project a soft boundary surface that spatially mediates between the first and second floors of the existing building. This soft boundary also links the inner space of the restaurant with the space defined by the famous roadside zelkova trees that symbolize the city of Sendai. Lights have been installed behind the inner wall, thereby pointillistically reconstructing the light and shade of the zelkova trees in the interior space.

The 2.3-millimeter-thick metal plates that constitute the inner wall were perforated by a numerically controlled turret with hundreds of thousands of variously sized holes. The pattern follows a digitized image of a zelkova tree that was decomposed and reassembled in Photoshop. Final adjustments to the graphic were done by hand by Atelier staff members. This process was done before the steel plates were folded into shape.

The inner wall is a monocoque structure that does not have any structural frames supporting it from behind. Therefore, the light passing through the graphic holes is not disrupted. Since there was no way to pierce graphic holes at the welded joint lines of the steel plates, the holes were marked again after assembly and welding and hand-drilled on-site.

The difficulty of welding complex shapes from thin steel plates within an existing building led to the use of shipbuilding technology for the actual manufacturing. Craftsmen who were highly experienced with the unique characteristics of steel plates were able to deform the steel freely by heating and chilling key points and thereby producing complex curved surfaces. The singular descriptive methods they used to translate a three-dimensional volume into two-dimensional surfaces were predicated on the manual craft techniques these experts used to make the curves.

ABOVE LEFT: Folded skin with perforations.
ABOVE RIGHT: Interior view.
BELOW LEFT: Unfolded skin with perforation pattern.
BELOW RIGHT: Detail of perforations.

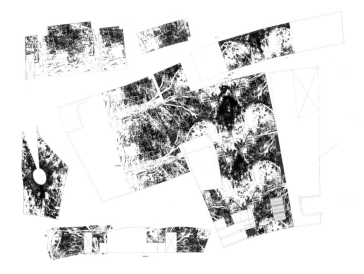

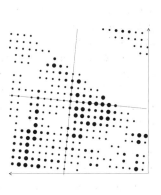

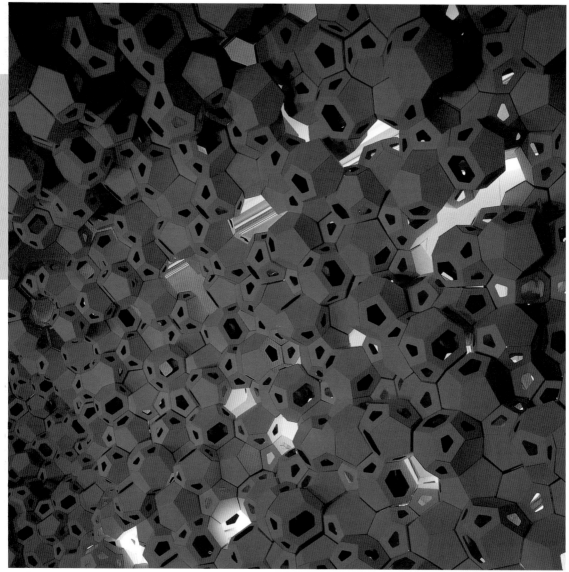

Digital Origami
University of Technology, Sydney/Chris Bosse, 2007

The aim of this project was to test the fitness of a particular module, copied from nature, to generate architectural space, operating from the assumption that the intelligence of the smallest unit dictates the intelligence of the overall system. Ecosystems such as reefs act as a metaphor for an architecture whereby the individual components interact in symbiosis to create an environment. In urban terms, the smallest homes—the spaces they create, the energy they use, the heat and moisture they absorb—multiply into a bigger organizational system, whose sustainability depends on their intelligence. From thirty-five hundred recycled cardboard molecules of only two different shapes, *Digital Origami* reinterprets the traditional concept of space.

CLOCKWISE FROM TOP LEFT: Exterior rendering of design; rendering showing nesting of two module types; interior rendering; unfolded modules; individual modules waiting for assembly on-site; module, second type; assembly; laser-cut modules from recycled cardboard.
BELOW: Completed installation.

C_Wall
Andrew Kudless/Matsys, 2006

C_Wall is the latest development in the architect's ongoing area of research into cellular aggregate structures. The project employs the Voronoi algorithm, a formula also used in a wide range of fields—such as satellite navigation, animal-habitat mapping, and urban planning—for its adaptability to local contingent conditions. In the case of *C_Wall*, the Voronoi algorithm facilitates the translation and materialization of information from particle simulations and other point-based data. Through this operation, points are transformed into volumetric cells, which can be unfolded, CNC-cut, and reassembled into larger aggregates. Built of thin paper and weighing very little, the structure exhibits an extremely high strength-to-weight ratio. In addition, the wall produces interesting patterns of light and shadow that are based on the differentiated pattern of cell sizes.

All photos: Francis Ware

Manifold
Andrew Kudless/Matsys, 2004

This research project develops a honeycomb system
that adapts to diverse performance requirements
through modulating the system's inherent geometric
and material parameters, while remaining within the
limits of available production technologies. *Manifold*
is based in the desire to form an integrated and
generative design strategy from a biomimetic
approach to architectural fabrication.

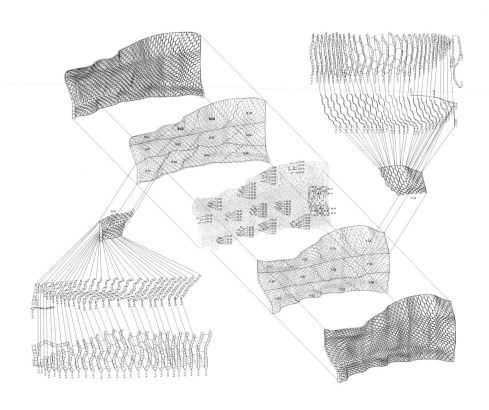

ABOVE: Exploded assembly diagram showing panelization and unfolded strips for front and rear surfaces.
BELOW: Completed installation.

Ruy Klein, *Tool-Hide*, 2006. Photo: Ruy Klein

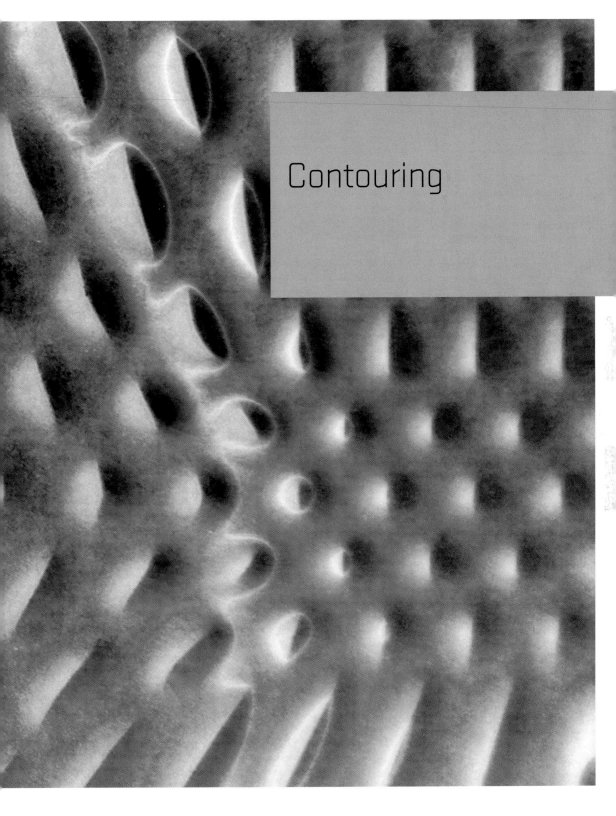

Contouring

Construction materials typically come as sheets. There are a host of building products that are smooth and flat: stone slabs, plywood, particleboard, MDF, gypsum board, and cast composites, among others. They may come in a range of thicknesses, but in essence they are two-dimensional surfaces. Contouring is a technique that reshapes this surface and creates a three-dimensional relief by removing successive layers of material. It is a subtractive process, akin to carving in regulated patterns.

There is a long history of such wood and stone carving in craft and architecture practice. Ordered Greek-column capitals, friezes, rock-cut architecture, Jain temples, and myriad other examples are testament to the productive aesthetic interface between carving and building. While the tradition of this technique is rich, it has nevertheless had limited application in architecture since the Industrial Revolution, largely because the hand and machine labor required to produce pieces is variable, limited by scale, and cost and time prohibitive.

Digital fabrication has enabled architects to transcend the idea that carving resides exclusively in traditional handcrafted practice. In fact, the notion of digital craft is rapidly gaining ground as a way to revive, using contemporary tools, the carved, ornamented, and articulated surface. These tools include CNC routers and mills, which use tool-path data derived from digital models to carve away material systematically as a series of contours. The tools are essentially computer-controlled versions of traditional wood- and metalworking equipment. Like their analog counterparts, CNC mills are commonly used for foams, wood, and soft metals such as aluminum and bronze.

There are several types of machines now commonly used in architecturally scaled projects. These include two-and-a-half-axis and three-axis CNC tools and, to a lesser extent, five-axis mills. The terminology of axes refers to the number of degrees of movement the machine is able to execute while cutting. The most common mill, for example—the three-axis mill—can move simultaneously in the X, Y, and Z directions. In other words, the cutting head can move in any plan configuration, as well as up and down simultaneously. This range of movement is generally more than adequate for most applications, since it can cut almost any pattern or relief from large sheet material. The essential difference between its capability and that of a machine with higher degrees of freedom is that the head on the three-axis mill does not rotate. Three-axis mills cannot, therefore, make undercuts or fully three-dimensional objects, whereas five-axis machines can. This additional range of movement is liberating, on the one hand, but in many instances not necessary. Architects have tended to develop inventive ways to work within the three-axis constraints. Moreover, the greater affordability, operability, size, and speed of these milling machines in comparison with more complex systems contribute to their widespread use.

Like other digital-fabrication techniques, CNC milling allows for a more fluid transition between computer model and physical construct. It also opens the door to numerous design and tooling possibilities. The process of contouring necessarily involves translating a digital model into a language a computer-controlled router can understand, and there are many commercial software packages that serve this purpose. The most common include Mastercam, RhinoCAM, and SURFCAM. In each case, the program asks the user to define a set of variables, among them the size and type of router bit, the material being cut, and the path of tool travel. Though the task might seem straightforward, there are literally thousands of ways to cut or contour an object. Tool paths can be parallel, spiral, smooth, ridged, sloped…. Deciding which method to use is a matter of coupling design intent with machine and material limitations.

Once the variables are specified, the software generates tool-path data in a programming language specific to CNC machines. This language, called G-code, lists the multiple operations for a particular job (spindle position, speed, depth, etc.) as a set of individual commands. Each command is listed on a separate line beginning with the letter G, giving the

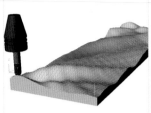

code its name. It is quite common for professional machinists to enter the routing process at the G-code stage and rewrite, alter, or insert new code to more carefully control the machine. Most architects, however, tend to use the more graphical interface provided by the milling software.

Contouring is by its very nature highly material and time intensive. As a subtractive fabrication process, CNC milling removes material from virgin sheets or blocks to make parts. Inherent to this process is material waste—sometimes a great deal—and at the same time the leftover material is invested with extreme design attention and labor. Consequently, contouring is consistently used by architects to elevate relatively ordinary building materials to extraordinary levels.

For example, the cover of Bernard Cache's book, *Earth Moves: The Furnishing of Territories*, depicts what could be a hilly contoured landscape.[1] In fact, it is a piece of laminated wood that has been carved with a CNC mill, or router. It was one of the first widely disseminated images of a digitally fabricated object that was compelling representationally at both the one-to-one and the architectural or landscape scales. The plywood laminations in the image read as striated contours, exposed by routing an undulating topography. In the book, Cache theorizes the application of Deleuzian folds in architectural practice—of outside and inside and across the scales of furniture, architecture, and geography. An architect and furniture designer, Cache uses representations of his projects as talking points for achieving subjective or inflected interpretations of objects. While he is not

dealing with digital technologies per se, he does argue for a nonstandard means of production to attain fluidity and variability in industrialized processes. In the chapter "Subjectile/Objectile," the six beautifully routed surfaces demonstrate his assertion that "digital machines and productive technologies in general allow for the production of an industrial continuum. From the mold we move toward modulation."[2] It was not lost on architectural designers that by leveraging digital contouring, one could transform the practice of making things, as well as create highly compelling surface effects.

Office dA's *Laszlo Files*, commissioned in 2001 for the Department of Architecture at the Harvard Graduate School of Design, is an early architectural example of digital fabrication that accentuates the sensuous properties of plywood with undulating contours. In this project, the plywood is laid on end so that the vertical edge grain reads against the elongated swells. The file pulls are seamlessly integrated into the overall geometry, routed out of the back side to provide a small opening for the hand. The contouring is smooth, allowing the material to provide the secondary texture.

Other architects have also experimented with using the routing process itself to generate surface texture. Greg Lynn, for instance, an architect whose work is largely identified with cultivating CNC processes, employs signature ridged tool paths. Homogeneous material becomes highly textural, so that the visual value of such pieces as the display for Prettygoodlife.com is not in the material itself but in the way it is milled. The rippled surface adapts

FROM LEFT:
Greg Lynn, Prettygoodlife.com
Showroom, Stockholm, Sweden, 2000.
Photo: Greg Lynn Form

Erwin Hauer, *Design I*, 1950.
Photo: Courtesy Erwin Hauer

Rapid-prototyping machine, Z-Corp
ZPrinter 310 Plus. Photo: Courtesy ZCorp

to accommodate hardware, as well as to create a dynamic sensuality in the wall.

As with Cache's work, these furniture-scale pieces are suggestive of much larger landscapes and building forms. In fact, contouring is often employed as an architectural model-making technique because it can closely match the smooth, fluid nature of NURBS forms and surfaces for building and landscape. Whereas other fabrication methods, such as tessellating and sectioning, offer ways to approximate and allude to these geometries, contouring offers the most direct and precise means to achieve them.

At the scale of building, however, it has not been adopted with the same alacrity as some of the other digital-fabrication methods have. It is not yet conceivable to produce a whole building by digitally carving it out of solid material. Contouring unique forms is also quite time intensive, and because the method is directly aligned with subtractive three-dimensional milling, it inevitably generates substantial material waste. This excessiveness has been well acknowledged, so architects have developed other ways to maximize the potential of contouring, such as milling molds for shaping planar materials. This technique, called forming, is the subject of the next chapter.

When limited by size and practicality, architects have expanded the use of contouring on smaller scales. In the case of Jeremy Ficca's *CNC Panels*, it is the tension between the material and normative tooling operations that yields new possibilities for material and visual performance. The entrance and exit paths of the required routing tool are used as a design device. The porous surface is made of a series of parallel cuts, articulated by the sloped ends of each routed aperture. The cuts celebrate the thickness of standard sheet material by revealing the inner plywood laminations.

Expanding this thread, WILLIAMSON WILLIAMSON's *Door with Peephole* and Ruy Klein's *Tool-Hide* begin with the tool constraints and work backward to generate surface texture and form. The driving element in *Door with Peephole* is, naturally, the peephole and its corresponding center seam, from which all the project's contours emerge. Rather than employ the standard parallel, spiral, or other packaged tool paths, the designers custom-defined the tool's path of travel and the corresponding markings of the router bit. *Tool-Hide*, by using a combination of radial and sinuous tool paths, similarly pushes the capabilities of CNC routing to generate a variegated texture akin to animal skin. SPAN's Matias del Campo and Sandra Manninger, meanwhile, used fluid tool paths to make connections across scale in *Gradient Scale*. The project is an armature to display architecturally scaled models, as well as an exhibition itself. By modifying the size and direction of the tool paths, similar patterns subtly alter to perceptually bridge scales.

Where these projects explore relationships of milling to surface, Urban A&O leverages three-axis CNC milling to execute a fully three-dimensional sculptural collection of forms for *Bone Wall*. The project is designed as a parametric array of modules, each of which transforms based on its position in the overall wall geometry. This geometry is governed by a set of longitudinal splines that attach to the modules at its vertices; to create this system, the design was modeled and developed in CATIA. In this case, the design revolves around a sophisticated module defined by its end vertices and connective internal splines. The arc of each spline is shaped by the relative positions of the end points. As the module is placed, or instantiated, across the wall, each internal spline adjusts to the size, thickness, and angle defined by these points, ultimately forming a unique geometry for each module within a family of similarly delineated elements.

The digital design process used for *Bone Wall* included outputting scaled models, in the form of three-dimensional prints, to assess overall form and test the relationship of modules to one another and to the whole. Three-dimensional printing and other forms of rapid prototyping (stereolithography, selective laser sintering, fused deposition modeling, and PolyJet) are now widely used methods of architectural model making. All of these systems use free-form technology to build physical models from stereolithography files, which can be readily produced from solid, or closed-surface, digital models, offering a compelling way to move from digital to physical modeling. Unlike full-scale construction, however, these systems do not address material or machine constraints. Such issues are considered during the fabrication phase.

To manufacture *Bone Wall*, each module was first systematically sliced in CATIA into thinner sections that corresponded to the allowable vertical dimension of the CNC router. This height, commonly called Z-axis travel, is determined by the space between the tool and the table. While routers can be made to have Z-axis travel of ten feet or more, most are designed for sheet material, making this figure far more limited—in this case, just several inches. The other machine limitation that had to be overcome was that three-axis routers can make only vertical plunges; they do not make undercuts. Therefore, realizing the three-dimensional form required routing both sides of each slice. While these technical limitations did not particularly sponsor greater development or refinement of the design, the tooling decisions required to control the direction and path of the cutting bit did.

Unlike Cache's wood surfaces or those of the *Laszlo Files*, the ultimate texture of *Bone Wall* is not smooth. Smooth surfaces require substantial finishing, usually by numerous additional passes with the machine and then sanding by hand afterward. The tool paths are intentionally revealed in *Bone Wall*. They are designed as a series of parallel passes, a relatively common way to rout out a surface yet here also quite effective as a way to bind the separate modules visually and accommodate their subtly changing geometries.

The projects that follow further test the limits of contouring for design. As Urban A&O did for *Bone Wall*, Erwin Hauer redefined the original form of *Design 306* to machine and material capabilities to physically develop and execute the project. Ironically, *Bone Wall* initially drew on Hauer's precast modular designs of the late sixties, while *Design 306*, done by Hauer in partnership with Enrique Rosado, in turn looks toward digital fabrication as a way to revisit the module and surface. It considers both the geometric limits of the instrumentation and subsequent tool-path markings as integral parts of the design. As all the projects in this chapter demonstrate, moving from digital to physical via computer-aided tools opens a gold mine of design opportunities for investigating the transitions between form, machine, and material.

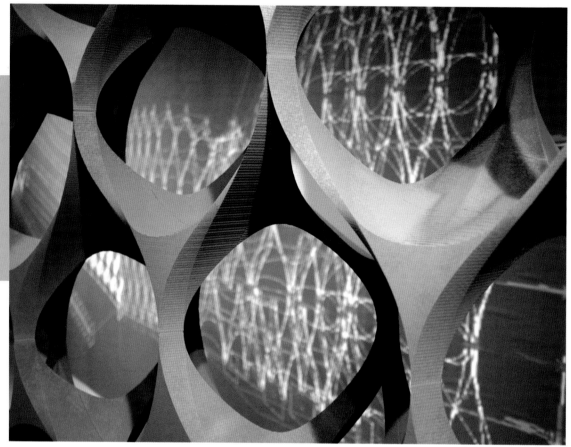

Bone Wall
Urban A&O, 2006

Inspired by the work of Austrian-born sculptor Erwin Hauer, the ambition of this experiment was continuity of surface and modulation of light within the wall, in addition to providing programmatic elements including storage and seating. The design of *Bone Wall* began with parametric modeling of a base "cell," or rather half cell, which was then inverted and rotated to combine into a complete cellular unit. The base cell has a total of eighteen corners, or "control points." Any change made to the geometry of the splines regenerates the shape of each cell, demonstrating both a nonlinear and reciprocal relationship between software and designer that is intrinsic to parametric, or parameter-based, modeling. A total of seventy-two cells—or 2,592 control points, all parametrically linked—combine to make up the wall.

The cells were fabricated in high-density foam on a five-axis CNC mill. On close inspection, the router's tool path can be seen on the surface of the wall: it is not entirely smooth to the touch. The milling machine was set on a $\frac{1}{32}$-inch step-over, resulting in a topographic planlike finish. The cells were then joined together by hand with adhesive, and the final wall was painted following assembly.

In its use of parametric modeling, *Bone Wall* is as an experiment toward the advancement of contemporary architectural practice. Parametric-modeling environments shape new cognitive ambiences within which design procedure is conceived. *Bone Wall* strives to demonstrate ornament's intrinsic necessity over extrinsic contingency.

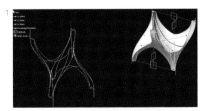

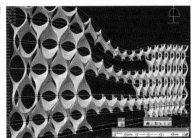

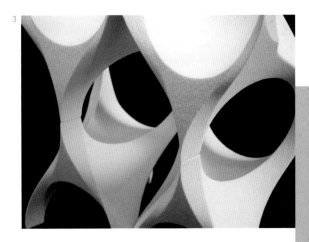

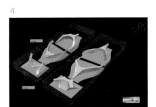

1 CATIA model of "powercopy."
2 CATIA screen grab describing instantiation of powercopy.
3 Scaled 3D print of portion of wall.
4 CATIA production model for routing modules in sections to fit Z axis of machine.
5 CNC routing of MDF modules.
6 Routed modules ready to be cut out from MDF block.
7 Assembly process.
8 Modules.
9 Wall assembly.
Photos: Joe MacDonald

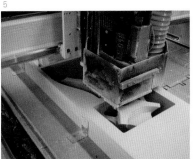

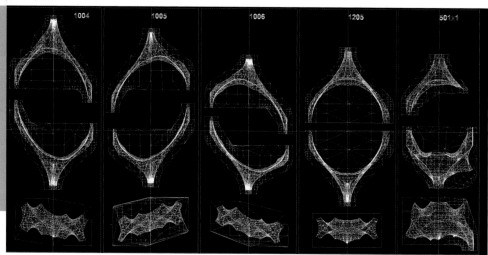

ABOVE: Drawing of sections for CNC routing of a single module.
BELOW: Details of foam cells.
Photos: Joe MacDonald

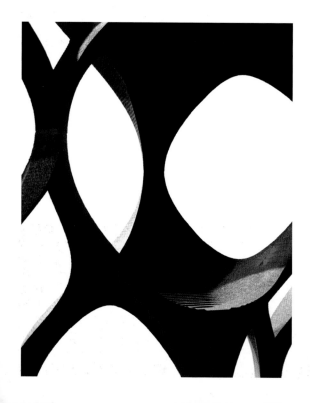

Views of completed project at Storefront for Art and Architecture. Photos: Stefan Hagen

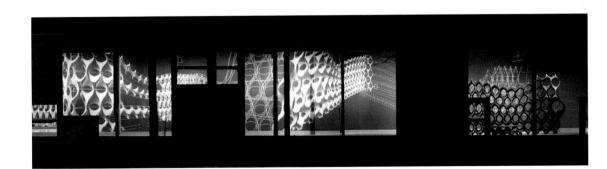

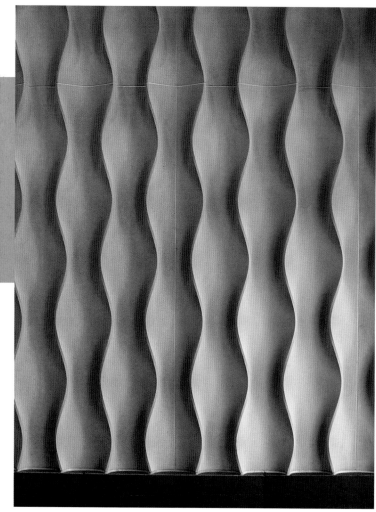

All photos: Courtesy Erwin Hauer

Design 306
Erwin Hauer and Enrique Rosado, 2005

Created in 2005, *Design 306* is a modification of *Design 6*, originally made in 1956. It is the result of a collaboration between Erwin Hauer and Enrique Rosado, and it was designed for the Centria, a new high-rise residential building within New York's Rockefeller Center.

Unlike its predecessor, *Design 306* was conceived for developing tool paths executed on a three-axis CNC mill, and it can be produced in a variety of materials. The first application, at the Centria, was made from Indiana limestone, but other stones and materials, such as MDF, may also be used. The size of the panels may vary to suit architectural needs and constraints. Panel sizes may be as large as ten feet by four feet, while the dimensions of the modules within the pattern are currently fourteen inches high by eleven inches wide. This ratio can be preserved, even as adjustments in scale are possible.

The design addressed an architectural situation in which transparency was undesirable but the modulation of light important. Perforations for the passage of light are therefore reduced to recessed, concave spaces.

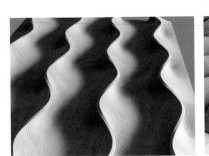

ABOVE: Freshly milled panel, single panel, installation on-site.
BELOW: Routed surface texture.

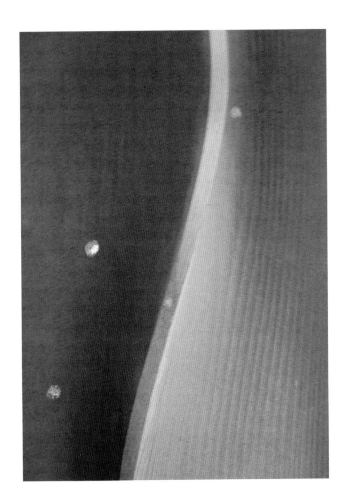

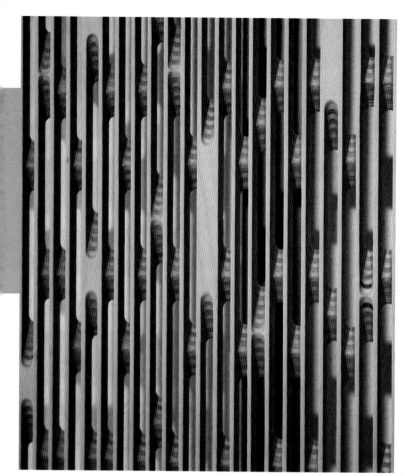

LEFT: Detail of CNC panel with graded entry and exit tool paths.
RIGHT: Installed CNC panel.
Photos: Jeremy Ficca

CNC Panels
Jeremy Ficca, 2004

Plywood is an affordable, widely available building material, utilized by the construction and furniture industries alike. This off-the-shelf product provided the palette for investigating of digital-fabrication techniques, specifically two-and-a-half-axis CNC routing, for which two-dimensional vector CAD drawings determined the tool paths. This plywood investigation produced a surface that could respond to the changing programmatic or environmental requirements of a given space, either through material mutability or built-in flexibility.

The general premise was to allow for the product to evolve through specific tooling investigations, the limits of which were largely dictated by the material itself. Seven-ply Baltic birch was chosen for its strength and finish quality. Initial routing was primarily two-dimensional, producing kerfs and cuts that allowed bending in response to push and pull, effectively transforming a rigid sheet into a pliable surface. A subtle change in the depth or spacing of kerfs dramatically affected the ease of bending and general stability. Milling too deep resulted in precarious sheets that were easily broken. Milling to shallow left the sheet rigidity effectively unchanged. As these investigations progressed, the milling moved to both faces of the plywood: the registration and intentional misregistration between cuts on both faces produced a lattice-like condition. At the scale of a room, the series of panels encourage a modulation of view and light.

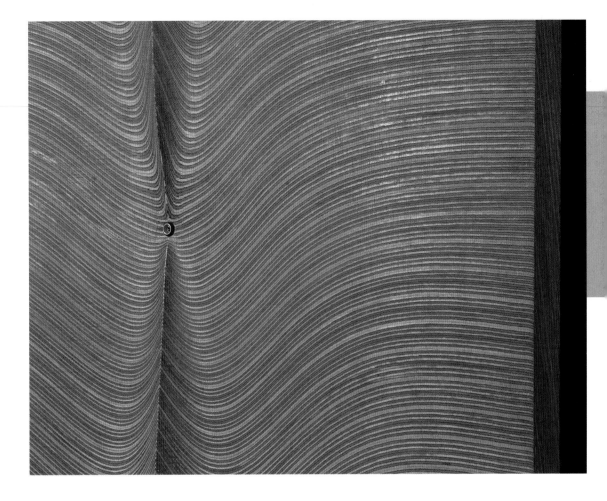

Door with Peephole
WILLIAMSONWILLIAMSON, 2004

This door is an investigation in three-dimensional patterning afforded by oblique laminate construction techniques and the subtractive process of CNC milling. The peephole is taken as an activation device across the space of the door, registering on either side its use or nonuse. Defining the inside, the peephole is pulled toward the viewing eye, while the geometric ridge is a barrier pulled sharply to the outside. This dialogue privileges the viewer with the ability to access the peephole and provides a geometric index of the orientation of use. Views of the door show the relationship of the oblique lamination to the resulting subtractive pattern that diagrams the orientation of the eye along the geometric spine and roughing passes.

Routing pattern.
Photos: John Howarth

Exhibition setup, models nested in surface.
Photos: SPAN

Gradient Scale
SPAN, 2005

Gradient Scale was conceived and built for the group exhibition "AustriArchitecture." The project explores issues of nonsequential scalar growth, surface articulation, and the panelization of a continuous nonrepeating surface using CNC fabrication methods. The design challenges the concept of scale in architecture and establishes a conceptual "digital-scape" as a testing ground for leaping scalar associations in viewing the exhibition.

To achieve a continuously growing scalar model, the architects developed an MEL script that repeated a series of five curves along the predefined length of the exhibition object. These curves were connected in Maya, creating a "bi-rail" surface. Through several iterations of forces influencing the surface, different degrees of articulations of the final element were created. The undulating surface can be read as a repetition of the one-to-one detail: the greater the frequency of the curves grows, the flatter the amplitude of the curves gets, resulting in a pattern that can be read as a texture in an urban scale.

Issues connected to digital production methods were explored using a three-axis milling machine. Using the milling software, SPAN calculated the tool paths to examine different surface patterns. These patterns emerged from the isoparms derived from the computational model. The final milled result was informed by consciously manipulating the isoparms, as well as by choosing different mill bits and varying the step sizes of the milling path. The jagging and rippling of the surface created reinforcement ribs in the panel's structure.

The problem of panelization was also explored in the production of *Gradient Scale*. The object, twenty feet long and five feet wide, was produced in three segments. Instead of forming straight, rectangular pieces, the cuts follow the model's isoparms, creating puzzle-like joints. Because the joints follow the NURBS's geometry, their formal appearance matches the entire project's language.

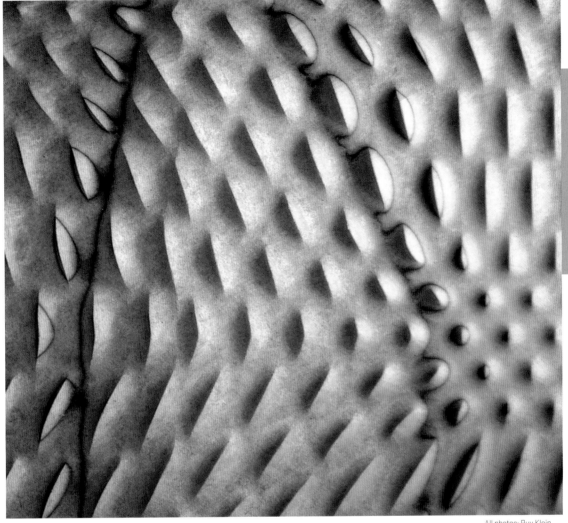

All photos: Ruy Klein

Tool-Hide
Ruy Klein, 2006

This project manipulates the technical limitations of CNC milling to produce ornamentation, using animal hides as a conceptual starting point. A set of four oversize closet doors were fabricated and then staggered in an overlapping pattern. The fabrication technique carefully managed the size of the router bit with a corresponding network of manipulated tooling paths to produce a cellular pattern of "scallops"— artifacts of a crude pass over the digitally formed surface geometry. Left unsanded, the tactile surface bore a texture akin to an elephant or iguana skin.

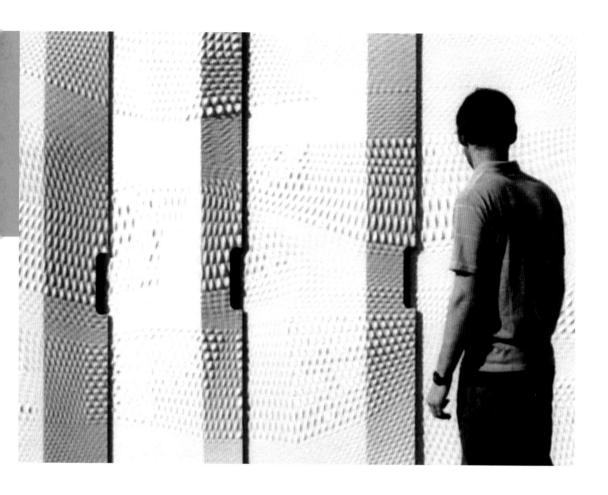

Concept related to iguana skin.

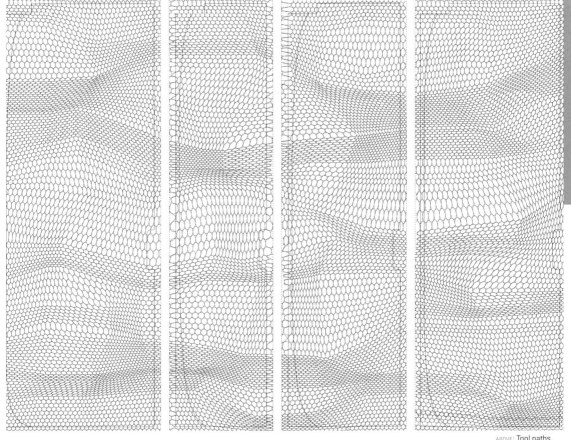

ABOVE: Tool paths.
BELOW: Surface sample tests.

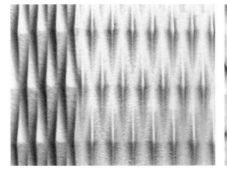

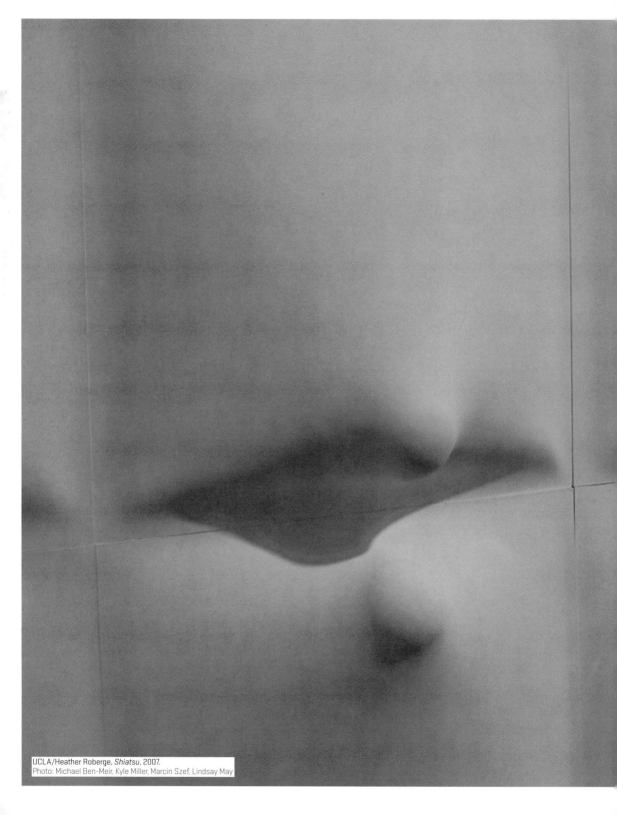

UCLA/Heather Roberge, *Shiatsu*, 2007.
Photo: Michael Ben-Meir, Kyle Miller, Marcin Szef, Lindsay May

Forming

Formed objects are all around us. Packaging, plastic toys, cell phones, car bodies….The list is virtually endless. Because forming employs an inherent economy of means—generating multiple parts from a small number of molds or forms—it follows that the most common uses for this technology are mass-produced products. In buildings, this falls into the realm of architectural components, such as hardware, facade panels, and window mullions. And of course, building construction also employs forming at a larger scale and with less reproducibility, for such components as precast panels, structural members, and architectural ornamentation, as well as cast-in-place slabs, walls, or even the whole building. All things considered, forming is ubiquitous in the construction industry.

Where most forming is relatively standard practice and used conventionally, of no particular architectural interest, there have certainly been a number of inspired projects and forming techniques developed throughout history. Examples include the precast facade panels and bas-reliefs especially popular in the 1960s, thin-shell structures, and uniquely formed cast-concrete buildings. It is beyond the scope of this book to discuss the great number of excellent cast-concrete buildings, but a few illustrative examples of manufactured building parts can provide some context for this fabrication technique.

Mass production influenced midcentury ideas of creating surface using formed elements. A fascination with such patterning can be found in the building designs of such well-established architects of the 1950s and '60s as Hans Scharoun and Harrison & Abramovitz, among others. These architects took advantage of industrial production to create highly detailed stamped-metal cladding units that could be arrayed across building facades in projects such as the Berliner Philharmonie and the Alcoa Building, respectively.

Precast panels also gained in popularity alongside the widespread use of concrete. Precasting offered immediate efficiency by reducing the amount of formwork necessary to make multiple parts. Many precast-panel applications resulted in relatively banal buildings, but there are notable exceptions. One is DMJM's American Cement Company Headquarters Building in Los Angeles, built in 1964. The two parts of the facade comprise highly sculptural formed panels that filter sunlight, screen the interior parking and office programs, and form a highly modeled surface at the street. The panels are reminiscent of and quite possibly influenced by Erwin Hauer's precast screens from a decade earlier.[1] Interestingly enough, Hauer, together with his partner Enrique Rosado, are now beginning to remake these designs using digital-contouring processes. Past or present, Hauer's experiments and others like them provide some of the most compelling arguments for the potential of precast concrete. The thinness of the concrete and delicacy of the screens belie the heaviness and solidity of the material. And the highly three-dimensional, sometimes intertwining configuration of the resulting surfaces would otherwise be nearly impossible to achieve.

As is the case, however, with most forms of mass production, the designed units of this time were necessarily identical and resulted in repetitive overall patterns. Though forming processes are never digital in themselves, digital fabrication has created new possibilities for conceiving and designing customizable formwork. It has had this liberating effect mostly because it cost-effectively produces nonstandardized mold making. For some applications, such as making stamped sheet-metal panels, the work and material to produce the dies is quite significant, and it is often unreasonable to manufacture unique dies for a limited use, such as for a single building. For many other forming methods, though, it is possible both to more effectively produce unique forms for single applications and molds and to make a range of parts in a variety of materials.

William Massie, a pioneer in the field of CAD/CAM architecture, conducted early experiments for producing formwork using a CNC router. As Coordinator for Building Technologies Research at Columbia University, Massie was immersed in the physical realities of making and pushed its digital

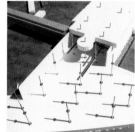

potential. Later, while teaching at the University of Montana, Massie honed in specifically on the tectonic potential of using the CNC router.

The concrete wall, the outcome of a research project, "Virtual Model to Actual Construct," represents Massie's initial foray, in 1997, into the process and one of the first architectural instances of making a full-scale built element using a computer-driven process.[2] The surfaces of the wall were first digitally modeled as warped planes. The model was then cross-sectioned into a series of profiles that corresponded to a ribbed formwork structure. Unlike typical formwork, which is built to the shape of the wall surface and removed after the concrete cures, these ribs were designed to stand crosswise and stay partially embedded in the structure once completed. The ribs, made of thin plywood, were perforated with a series of edge slots for threading long acrylic slats. The acrylic pieces, though flat, were thin and flexible enough to cumulatively approximate the curved shape of the wall surface. A series of larger holes cut into the center of each rib allowed the wet concrete mix to pass from one section to the next, structurally binding the wall together. The formwork ribs were easily snapped off

once the concrete cured, leaving the acrylic sheets to be peeled off as a final step. What is striking about this project—other than that the rib profiles were made with a computer-controlled router from data obtained directly from the digital model—is that it necessitated innovating a formwork strategy. That is, the particulars of the digital method forced Massie to revisit a standard construction practice and design a new one—one that offered its own aesthetic potential.

Big Belt House, a residence Massie designed and built for himself in the foothills of Montana's Big Belt Mountains in 1999, demonstrates a variation on the technique he used for the concrete wall. In this case, the curved ribs of the house were cast in CNC-routed foam molds, puzzle-fit together on-site, then spanned with PVC tubing. Once the form was achieved, the tubes were shot with concrete slurry and trowelled to a smooth finish. While this construction process is highly atypical, the precision obtained by first digitally modeling the site, then producing the design and subsequent formwork from the three-dimensional digital data, eliminated the need for traditional construction drawings and reduced related on-site errors. Most important, it offered

William Massie, "Virtual Model to Actual Construct," 1997.

CLOCKWISE FROM TOP LEFT:

Digital model of wall; CNC-routing formwork rib; formwork rib; finished wall; removing exterior formwork; casting process; assembled formwork.

Photos: William Massie

a way to build the supple form of the building as an integrated digital process.

On a much larger scale, Gehry Partners was one of the first, in 2000, to employ CNC-milled formwork as a constructional method for making a precast concrete wall.[3] For the Zollhof Towers in Düsseldorf, Styrofoam blocks were digitally routed to make 355 unique cast-concrete molds, each of which was routed around specific window openings, laid with steel rebar, then filled with concrete to make the structural wall panels. The final undulating building form is the direct result of this process. In their respective projects, Massie and Gehry both investigate digital forming at the scale of building by innovating formwork for cast concrete. Since Massie and Gehry forged the way, a host of other forming techniques commonly used in industrial and product design are now being adopted for architecture by a younger generation of designers.

Industrial design has had a far longer history of employing digital tools and has the advantage of having always used formwork for mass production. This formwork, more commonly referred to as "molds" or "forms," is made using digital milling

and sometimes rapid-prototyping machines, and then is used to cast repetitive parts. Such forming processes involve the use of both negative (female) and positive (male) molds. The processes that employ female molds include casting, vacuum and thermo forming, and injection and rotor molding. Vacuum and thermo forming are also commonly used with male molds, and both male and female sides are sometimes used together for stamping metal and other similar processes. Because a large number of final parts is generated from a single mold, it is not surprising that a lot of time, expense, and design innovation go into the making of the mold.

Forms are ultimately a means to an end. They may or may not look like the final product. In the Ost/Kuttner Apartment, KOL/MAC created fluid, smooth surfaces using sectioned plywood formwork. This project, built in 1997, was one of the first to move effectively from the smooth surfaces of the digital model into physical form. To accomplish this, the architects used a process similar to that for making boats or surfboards, both of which commonly employ resin-coated fiberglass fabric over shaped molds. For the apartment, the mold was made using a sectioned

structure and inserted urethane foam pieces. The fiberglass was laid over, sanded smooth, and coated with a tinted epoxy resin akin to the final gel coats on boats, yielding the flowing, liquidlike surface.

While KOL/MAC's forms were in this case unique to the part and integral to the final structure, architects are working with ways to leverage mold making to produce variation without sacrificing an economy of means. This effort most often implies that molds are used repetitively, but it can also imply different relationships between part and mold or investigations into what forming can produce as a constructional system. Included in this chapter are projects that align such constructional efficiencies with design intent.

In the *Prototype Pavilion* by MOS, the highly elaborate milled foam formwork remains a semistructural and constructional part of the final project, covered by hand-laid fiberglass below and sheet metal above. It essentially forms a sandwich panel where the high degree of surface undulation is coupled with structural performance; the undulations allow the panel to span without sagging. *UniBodies*, a series of prototypes by PATTERNS's Marcelo Spina, in collaboration with the fabrication studio Kreysler & Associates, also employs hand-laid fiberglass over CNC-milled urethane foam to produce structural skins. Unlike *Prototype Pavilion*, however, the monocoque structure is achieved purely through the form of the molded part. As they do in folding, shaping and bending sheet materials provide inherent structure. *UniBodies* takes cues from automobile body parts, which are lent rigidity from integral surface

deformations. The sheer thinness of the fiber-reinforced polymer contests the stiffness achieved, and each construction resonates between subdivided structure and singular whole.

While these two projects look at the structural performance of form and material, other projects included here draw out the sensual properties of forming. Vacuum-formed installations by GNUFORM, servo, and SPAN balance the use of repetitive and unique molds to make overall figural pieces, ultimately drawing associations with bio- and zoomorphic creatures. *NGTV* by GNUFORM, for example, takes on animalistic characteristics at its furry seams. The design comprises nine glowing, translucent panels, each formed with inverted clamshell-like ridges that provide stiffness, create thickness and shadow, and further its association with living things.

Whereas *NGTV* efficiently uses the same molds to form sets of identical panels, servo developed a limited collection of forms that could ultimately produce a variable kit of parts. "Dark Places," an exhibition designed by servo for seventy-six artists at the Santa Monica Museum of Art, is a sinuous set of strands suspended in the gallery space. The strands are composed of eight to eleven interlocking segments that enable the strands to subtly change shape. With only five different part types, the whole takes on an organic, serpentlike quality through simple rotation and transposition of elements.

The "Housing in Vienna" exhibition by SPAN takes the concept of modularization a step further. The multiple displays were made of a single unit comprising three vacuum-formed layers. The

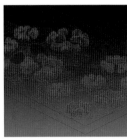

FROM LEFT:

Sidewalk in Cairo featuring pentagonal
Cairo tessellation. Photo: Craig Scott

Florencia Pita, *Alice*, 2007. SURFCAM tool
paths, four-by-eight-foot bounding box
for wall piece. Photo: Florencia Pita

Alice. SURFCAM screen shot of wall piece.
Photo: Florencia Pita

project uses a pentagonal Cairo tessellation pattern, flexibly aggregated to yield multiple overall arrangements. Each vertical layer of the cell was formed using CNC-milled molds, and the resulting shells fit together like a plastic container. The parts were rigid, thin, light, and easily transportable. In short, the project blurs the boundary between architecture and industrial design. It begins with a strategy at the scale of fabrication, in this case using a CNC router and vacuum former, and develops into something architecturally scaled through multiplication. At the same time, each unit is invested with intricate surface detail and "formal economies"—forms that provide local programmatic and structural performance.

The work of Heather Roberge and her students at UCLA is also designed with an eye toward repetition and difference through a limited series of modules. With *Satin Sheet*, a single hexagonal tile creates multiple configurations through a simple rotation into six positions. The six edges of the tile are designed to match every other in plan and section. Hence the internal ridges, swells, and valleys form continuous lines that sinuously snake through the whole in a variety of patterns. *Shiatsu*, by contrast, uses a set of three jigs to produce a variety of related parts. The project employs superforming, a process used to make auto-body parts: an aluminum sheet is heated to 450–500 degrees centigrade and then forced into shape with air pressure. In *Shiatsu*, the aluminum sheet is shaped by the form of the jig surface, a ribbed insert, and controlling the location of the air pressure. The project expands the technique of superforming,

creating a voluptuous surface through an efficient material process.

Alice, an installation by Florencia Pita, explores the relationship of repetitive parts to singular wholes as a way to generate variety from a limited taxonomy of parts. The project uses both male and female molds and techniques of casting and vacuum forming to achieve its two complementary botanical pieces. The fabrication process began by deriving tool paths from digital models of the flowerlike shapes. The digital model, made in Maya, was first imported into machining software (in this case, SURFCAM) to specify the method and sequence by which the material was to be cut. This step included defining the diameter of the tool bits, whether the pass would be a rough, medium, or finishing one, and finally the travel path of the router. In some cases, the routing pattern—parallel, spiral, pocketing, and so forth—is intentionally visible in the final material and becomes an integral part of the design. For *Alice*, since the milled formwork underwent a secondary process to make the actual molds, and the design sought a smooth, shiny finish, the routing pattern was designed to be relatively refined without being excessively finished. The steps used for this process were essentially the same as those for contouring; however, the resulting milled form was used for mold making rather than serving as the final object.

The milled formwork was then used in two ways. For the outer "flowers," a layer of vinyl PVC was vacuum-formed over the routed sheet of lightweight MDF, an ideal material for this application, since it is simultaneously rigid and porous. It is also dense enough to retain a high level of detail during the milling process, yet it allows air to pass through evenly for vacuum forming. The PVC then became the female mold for the series of cast flower halves. This material was also well suited to its application here, because it can take and hold a detailed shape yet is flexible enough to release the forms once they are cured. The pieces were later fitted together to make complete three-dimensional forms. For the second method, the orange vacuum-formed vinyl became the finished panel. The two parts—panel and flower—fit together to form a surreal garden. *Alice* is strategic in its use of replication and mirroring to produce overall variety with limited elements.

Forming is a rich territory for architects today; it encompasses a wide array of standard industrialized processes and can be coupled with numerous materials and analog- and digital-fabrication methods. *P_Wall* by Andrew Kudless is digitally conceived and designed, but the construction is purely analog. The reconfigurable fabric mold is loosely controlled by pegs set at different positions and heights, but the fabric is ultimately allowed to settle naturally when filled with wet plaster. The crevices, creases, and bulges that result evoke resonances with organic bodies, unable to be replicated mechanically or digitally. This and the other projects included in this chapter produce synthetic effects that far outweigh the individual components. They perhaps have the greatest application for architecture at a larger scale and speak to the richness of this technique for building in a digital age.

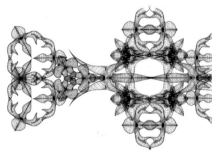

Early study of ornamental panel.
All photos: Florencia Pita

Alice
Florencia Pita mod, 2007

Alice is an installation that takes its form from a tale; its name comes from a narrative that creates multiple fictional landscapes. There is no literal relationship between the installation and the original story by Lewis Carroll; the aim is instead to capture the sensibility and atmosphere of the story and to endow the space with it. Much of the aesthetic of the piece is related to the images created by illustrators who used both highly detailed black-and-white engravings to accentuate shallow depth with frontally oriented two-dimensional graphics and later illustrations that introduce mood through color.

Alice focuses on these ideas of figuration and color. Figuration is developed as a way to exaggerate form, to capture very specific geometric notations of given objects and manipulate them, a kind of exacerbated embellishment of curvaceous form. Color allows for the manipulation of materiality and space, such that certain materials have a coded color condition that defines their character. The project intends to accentuate materiality's character by exalting its pigmentation. The material is plastic and the color is orange; the idea was that the right sensibility for the object should be similar to that of a plastic toy: you see how the parts lock, and you have the urge to touch it. The work resides within an aesthetic of densely ornamented form that returns to a realm of embellishment and fantasy.

1

2

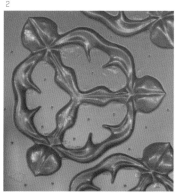

3

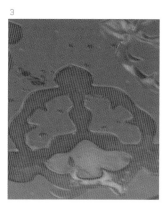

4

5

1 CNC-milled MDF formwork, base mold for vacuum-formed mold for cast units.

2 Vacuum-formed sixteenth-inch Styrene mold for cast units.

3 Urethane cast on vacuum-formed molds.

4 Cast units.

5 CNC-milling positive formwork for vacuum-formed cladding.

6 Vacuum-forming process, heating eighth-inch PETG previously laminated on orange vinyl.

7 Test prototype of joint between cast units and wall piece.

8 Installation at LAXART, Culver City, California.

6

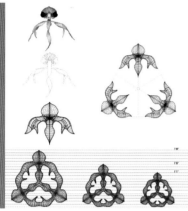

ABOVE: Description of design process of typical unit.
BELOW LEFT: Diagram of cast unit attachment.
BELOW RIGHT: Detail of completed installation.

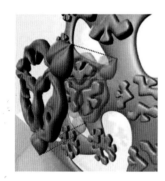

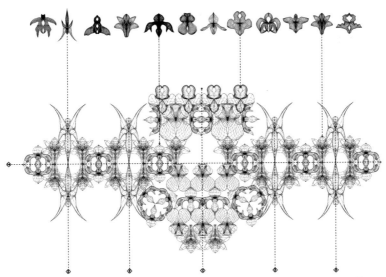

ABOVE: Diagram of assembly of flower units.
BELOW: Completed installation at LAXART.

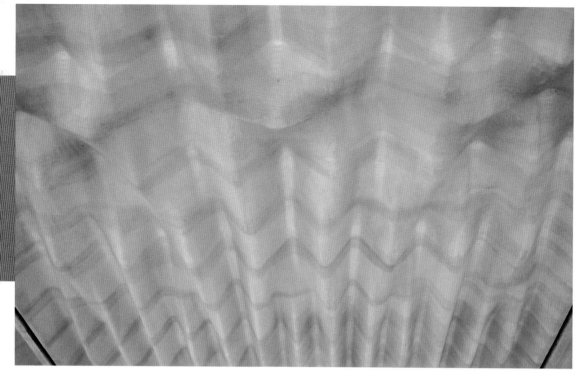

All photos: MOS

Prototype Pavilion
MOS, 2005

This prototype pavilion was designed and built to research experimental structural systems, particularly stiffness, through corrugation and branching. The focus of the design was researching CNC-manufactured fiberglass stress-skin roof panels that attempt to resolve two seemingly incommensurate conditions: translucency and load-bearing structure.

For the stress-skin panels, the removal of material reduced mass and increased the structural surface area. The corrugation offered an advantage of load transfer over a flat sheet panel. The designed branching allowed for even further distribution of stress loading. By keeping the system finite—by keeping the formal constraints fixed—the operation of material restructuring was acquired through continual cellular subdivision.

The initial corrugation pattern was acquired by spacing wave patterns of varying frequencies at a constraint equivalent to the material depth. The Fibonacci sequence was employed proportionately along the length. To increase the effect of the branching from panel to panel, a scalar technique was employed: the wave patterns were projected along a parabolic curve that described the length of two panels, one panel, or half of a full panel. The resulting curves were used to generate the final panel-branching forms.

The core of the stress-skin panel is three-inch-thick, two-pound lightweight EPS foam. The intent was to allow light to pass through at its thinnest points. It is surfaced with several layers of fiberglass composite of varying materials and weights. To increase the bonding of the composite, the panels were vacuum treated. Although the stress-skin panels have not been fully tested, the design process included several preliminary and empirical loading tests. Ultimately, the goal is that this lightweight, corrugated, panelized system be further developed into a panelized hybrid structural enclosure system of increased performance.

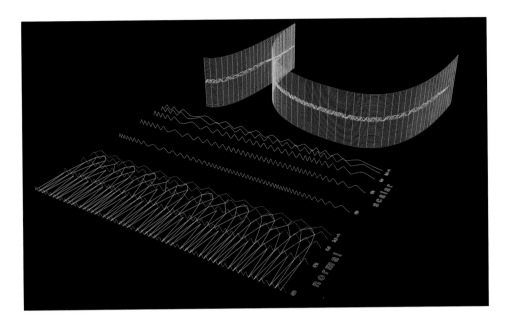

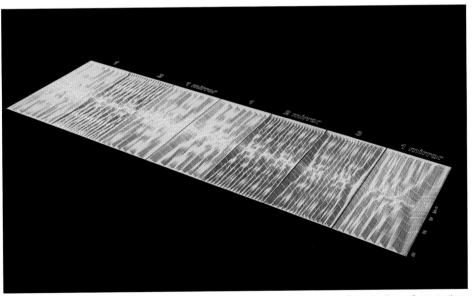

TOP: Generative diagram for corrugations.
BOTTOM: Three-dimensional corrugations.

FROM LEFT: Milled-foam substrate; panels of milled-foam substrate; laying fiberglass over milled-foam substrate.
BELOW: Underside of canopy.
OPPOSITE: Assembled canopy.

UniBodies
PATTERNS, with Kreysler & Associates, 2006

UniBodies is a collaborative project driven by PATTERNS's ongoing design research on shell structures and their impact on architectural form and tectonics. Also informed by the expertise of a composite forming company, Kreysler & Associates, *UniBodies* conceptually investigates the potentiality of composite shells in producing small and intensive proto architectures. These architectures inventively challenge the implicit distinctions between skeleton and skin, modular and monolithic, smooth and porous while pursuing an advanced degree of technological, formal, and material invention.

Materially, *UniBodies* investigates the plasticity of composites and unitized construction systems. Composites, or FRPs (fiber-reinforced polymers), have the capacity to synthetically subsume systems,

melding, fusing, and embedding discrete components within single-body shells. Furthermore, composites imply an amalgamation of time and procedure. Based on a unique use of anisotropic components to heterogeneously assemble surfaces, every piece is made entirely of a variable combination of fiber cloth, resin matrix, and flexible core materials. *UniBodies* exploits the versatility of composites to produce artificial materialities and intensive gradients. Variable degrees of translucency, viscosity, and surface profile are integrally molded and explored through pigmentation and filling of the resin.

Finally, *UniBodies* is as much about the cohesive material sensation and intimacy within these physical bodies as it is about the potential to induce resonances between those bodies and the human body.

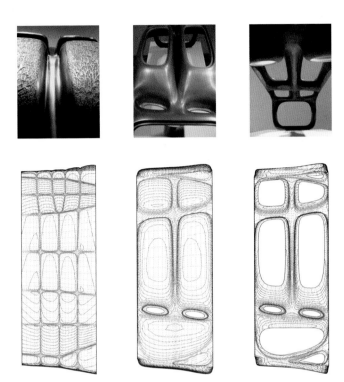

ABOVE: Surface details, surface contour of shells.
BELOW: Completed integral ribbed shell.

Photo: Deborah Bird

NGTV
GNUFORM, 2005

Designed as part of a larger project for the new
No Good Television Headquarters in Beverly Hills,
the private bar is the heart of a heavy, sensual
atmosphere created throughout the building
through rich color and light. Materials, effects,
and techniques used more sparingly in other areas
of the project come together in the bar to form an
enriched core, which is used as a reception area
for guests, a set for celebrity interviews, and a
standard bar for frequent company parties. It is
atmospheric infrastructure.

GNUFORM's earlier work involving hirsute
morphology led to, among other things, an interest
in constructing furry edges between and within
individual panels and between the bar and the curtains
beyond. Hazy edges are produced within a panel
when light passes through acutely curved surfaces.
The intense curvatures force the light to fall off before
it illuminates the actual edge of the material. This
falloff is shaped by the surfaces such that the light
appears more coherent than ambient illumination
yet less defined than the plastic edges themselves.

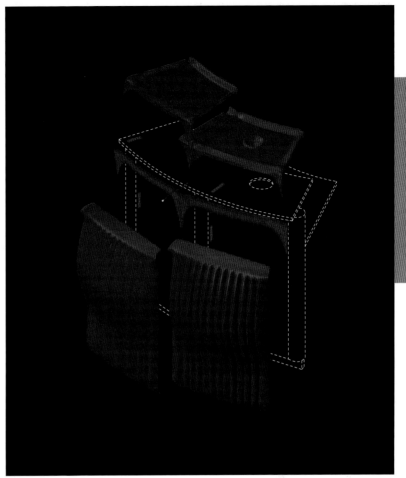

ABOVE: Diagram for assembly of panels. Photo: GNUFORM
BELOW: Diagram of sensorial cues.

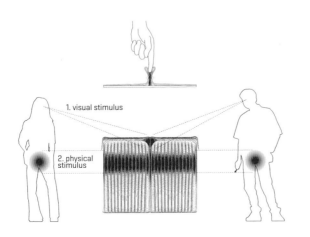

1. visual stimulus

2. physical stimulus

"Dark Places"
servo, 2006

The "Dark Places" exhibition distributes seventy-six selected artworks through four woven-together plastic strands, each containing different types of projections. These form three environments as each strand torques into alignment with its neighbor. In addition, a large-format front projection peels off of the outer perimeter of the gallery space; a collection of floating "cinematic objects" is rear-projected at head height and grouped into two clusters in the space. All biographical information about the artists is contained in four touch screens that are rooted in the ground, shooting upward into the strands, where visitors activate the system and stimulate lighting effects that span the space at-large.

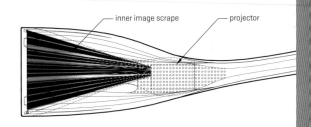

inner image scrape   projector

ABOVE: Diagram of image scrape.
BELOW: Detail showing image scrape.

ABOVE: **Detail of touch-screen interface.** Photo: servo
BELOW LEFT: **Production of canopy units during installation; section drawings.** Photo: servo
BELOW RIGHT: **Section drawings.**
OPPOSITE: **Completed project at Santa Monica Museum of Art.** Photo: Erdman Photography

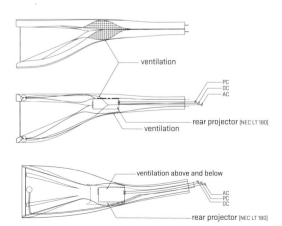

Photos: SPAN

"Housing in Vienna"
SPAN, 2007–8

This "pod family" was designed for the traveling exhibition "Housing in Vienna." It demonstrates a clear evolution of the pod as it includes the creation of limbs evolving out of the shell-shaped system. Just three surfaces build up one pod. The pod form is derived from the Cairo tessellation, whose inherent geometry allows it to repeat in multiple ways, thus creating manifold possibilities for assembling the exhibition in various given environments without compromising the overall appearance of the design.

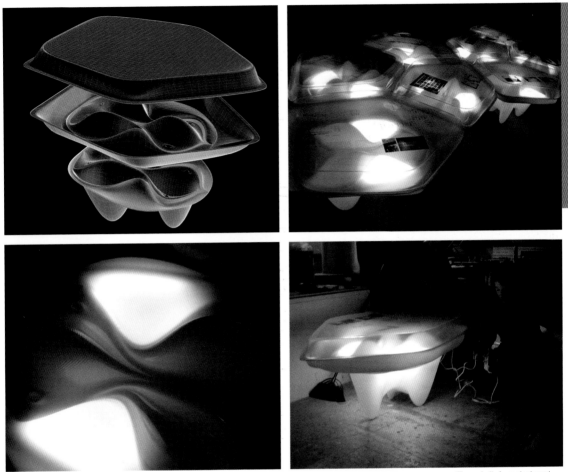

TOP LEFT: **Three shells form single pod.**
TOP RIGHT: **Mobile-exhibition "colony of pods."**
BOTTOM: **Illumination tests with vacuum-formed prototype.**

Illustrators: Miguel Alvarez, Daniel Carper, Alissa Hisoire, Carrie Smith

Satin Sheet
University of California, Los Angeles/
Heather Roberge, 2007

By aggregating one panel shape as a tessellated field, variation in multiple panel orientations renders an immense number of organizational possibilities. The intentional use of a hexagonal panel maximizes the combination of abutting sides and exhausts the rotational capacity of a single shape. The articulation of field line work within the homogeneous shape allows the project to develop field effects that materialize from multiple panel combinations. Two panels were developed to achieve varied field effects. This set of panel morphologies subtly differs in the textural and surface shading but remains completely analogous to the hexagonal boundary and side profile.

The optical effect of this strategy generates an aqueous grain that seamlessly transitions between conditions of laminar flow and turbulence throughout the field; it is similar to the effect of water or the swirling of clouds. As a result of this continuous transition between panels, the seams of the rigid hexagonal shape dissolve into the dominant surface grain, allowing the field effects of the tessellated panel to emerge.

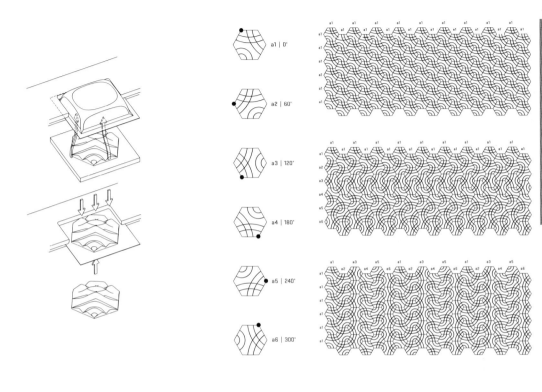

a1 | 0°

a2 | 60°

a3 | 120°

a4 | 180°

a5 | 240°

a6 | 300°

ABOVE: Diagram of superform process;
tessellation strategies based on tile rotation.
BELOW: Final pattern.

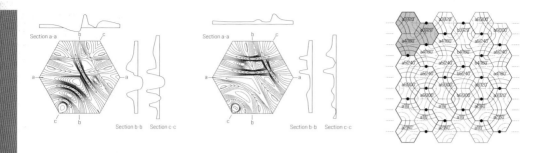

ABOVE: **Plan and sections of final two tile patterns; diagrams of built portion of overall final pattern and tile rotation.**
BELOW: **Completed installation.**
Photo: Lindsay May Photographs

Photo: Lindsay May Photographs

Shiatsu
University of California, Los Angeles/
Heather Roberge, 2007

Shiatsu challenges conventional superform-technology processes by employing the concept of variable pressure to produce panel variation and, ultimately, field complexity. Locally controlling the forming process achieves maximum variation through minimal production of molds. For this research, *Shiatsu* employed three jigs, brought together in one tool over which aluminum could be formed. Whereas conventional forming produces one panel type through one mold, this tool can literally produce hundreds of thousands of panel types by converting the process of superform into a highly controlled art. *Shiatsu* unearths a previously dormant capability of superforming aluminum and introduces a new process from which architectural componentry can be made at maximum variety and minimal cost. The variety of the end product allows for endless configurations and substrate mappings, rather than reproduction, thus further validating the use of variable pressure forming.

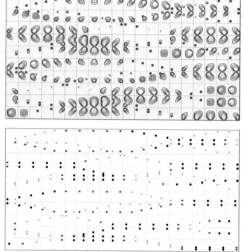

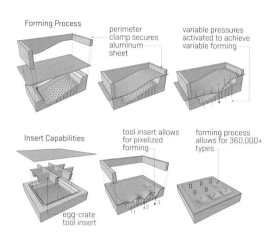

Forming Process

perimeter clamp secures aluminum sheet

variable pressures activated to achieve variable forming

Insert Capabilities

tool insert allows for pixelized forming

forming process allows for 360,000+ types

egg-crate tool insert

ABOVE: **Panel contours and pressure points; forming process.** Illustrators: Michael Ben-Meir, Kyle Miller, Marcin Szef
BELOW: **Tile-forming process.**

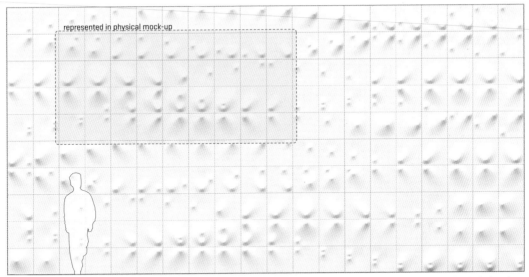

represented in physical mock-up

ABOVE: Final pattern with call-out for physical mock-up.
Illustrators: Michael Ben-Meir, Kyle Miller, Marcin Szef
BELOW: Completed installation.
Photo: Lindsay May Photographs.

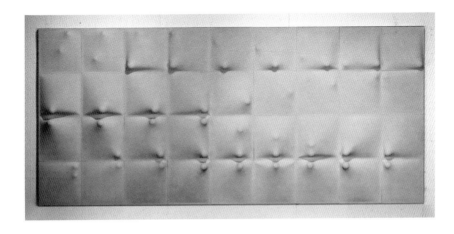

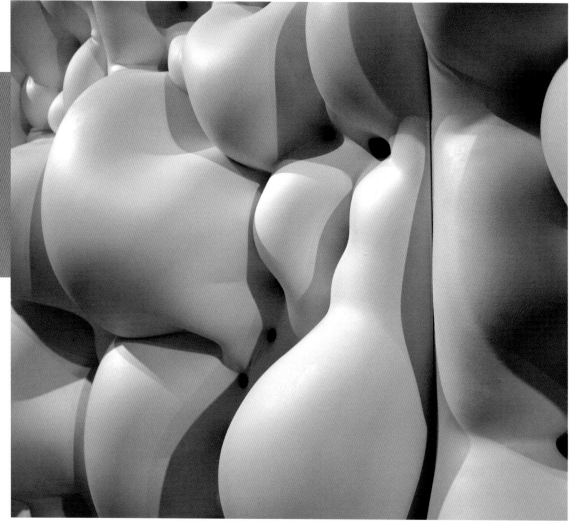

All photos: Andrew Kudless

P_Wall
Andrew Kudless/Matsys, 2006

P_Wall investigates the self-organization of two
materials—plaster and elastic fabric—to produce
evocative visual and acoustic effects. Inspired by the
work of the Spanish architect Miguel Fisac and his
experiments with flexible concrete formwork in the
1960s and '70s, *P_Wall* attempts to continue this
line of research and add to it the ability to generate
larger and more differentiated patterns. The plaster
tiles have a certain resonance with the body as it sags,
expands, and stretches in its relationship with gravity
and structure.

ABOVE: Scripted diagram of formwork points.
BELOW: Completed installation.

Notes

Introduction

1. Robin Evans, "Translations from Drawing to Building," in *Translations from Drawing to Building and Other Essays* (Cambridge: MIT Press, 1997).
2. Branko Kolarevic, "Information Master Builders," *Architecture in the Digital Age: Design and Manufacturing* (New York: Spon Press, 2003), 57.
3. Jim Glymph, "Evolution of the Digital Design Process," in Kolarevic, *Architecture in the Digital Age*, 101–20.
4. Michael Speaks, "Design Intelligence and the New Economy," *Architectural Record* (January 2001).

Sectioning

1. Le Corbusier, *Ronchamp*, trans. Jacquelaine Cullen (Stuttgart: Verlag Gerd Hatje, 1957), 92.
2. Greg Lynn, *Animate Form* (New York: Princeton Architectural Press, 1999), 18.
3. Cecil Balmond, *Serpentine Gallery: Pavilion 2005 Designed by Alvaro Siza, Eduardo Souto De Moura with Cecil Balmond, Arup* (London: Serpentine Gallery, 2005).
4. Douglas Gauthier, "BURST* 2007," MoMA submission booklet, 2007.

Tessellating

1. Peter Macapia, "Turbulent Grid. Dirty Geometry (part 1)," *arch'it*, February 6, 2007, http://www.architettura.it.
2. Ibid. See also Peter Macapia, "Dirty Geometry," *Log10* (Summer–Fall 2007): 137–51.
3. Achim Menges, "Polymorphism," in *Architectural Design, Techniques and Technologies in Morphogenetic Design*, ed. Michael Hensel, Achim Menges, Michael Weinstock (London: Wiley Academy, 2006), 79–87.
4. See Fabio Gramazio and Matthias Kohler, *Digital Materiality in Architecture* (Baden, Switzerland: Lars Müller Publishers, forthcoming).

Folding

1. Greg Lynn, "Architectural Curvilinearity: The Folded, the Pliant, and the Supple," *Folding in Architecture*, ed. Greg Lynn (London: Architectural Design Magazine, 1993), 8.
2. Heinrich Engel, *Structure Systems* (New York: Frederick Praeger, 1968).
3. Farshid Moussavi and Michael Kubo, eds., introduction to *The Function of Ornament* (Barcelona: Actar, 2006), 5–12.
4. See Michael Hensel and Achim Menges, eds., *Morpho-Ecologies: Towards Heterogeneous Space in Architecture Design* (London: Architectural Association, 2006).
5. Tom Wiscombe, excerpt from *Dragonfly* project text.

Contouring

1. Bernard Cache, *Earth Moves: The Furnishing of Territories*, ed. Michael Speaks, trans. Anne Boyman (Cambridge: MIT Press, 1995).
2. Ibid.

Forming

1. See Erwin Hauer, *Continua: Architectural Screens and Walls* (New York: Princeton Architectural Press, 2004).
2. William Massie, "Virtual Model to Actual Construct: A Direct Link to Computer-Generated Formwork," *Architecture* 87, no. 4 (1998): 98.
3. Jim Glymph, "Evolution of the Digital Design Process," in *Architecture in the Digital Age: Design and Manufacturing*, ed. Branko Kolarevic (New York: Spon Press, 2003), 101–20.

Sectioning

Digital Weave, University of California, Berkeley/
Lisa Iwamoto, 2004
DESIGNERS: Lisa Iwamoto (faculty), Josh Beck, Aaron Brumo,
Kristi Dykema, Mike Eggers, Aaron Korntreger, Ursula Lang,
Danny Lee, Lih-Chiun Loh, Myrto Milou, Heather Moore,
Sam O Meara, Margaret Sledge, Meredith Weems, Yantien Wong
LOCATION: SFMOMA Contemporary Extension (CX),
"Atmosphere" furniture store, San Francisco, California
SOFTWARE: Rhinoceros, AutoCAD
MATERIAL: 4mm Coroplast
FABRICATION: Water-jet cutter

Mafoombey, Martti Kalliala, Esa Ruskeepää,
with Martin Lukasczyk, 2005
DESIGNERS: Martti Kalliala and Esa Ruskeepää, with
Martin Lukasczyk
LOCATION: Helsinki, Finland
SOFTWARE: Rhinoceros
MATERIAL: 7mm corrugated cardboard
FABRICATION: Die-less cutting and creasing table

(Ply)wood Delaminations, Georgia Institute of Technology/
Monica Ponce de Leon, 2005
DESIGNERS: Monica Ponce de Leon (faculty), Asa Martin,
Richard Aeck, Paul Ehret
TEAM: Thomas Dinatale, Leonard Lowrey, Minh Nguyen,
Benton Carper, Jennifer Smith, Austin Hall, Tim Olmstead
LOCATION: Georgia Institute of Technology, Atlanta, Georgia
SOFTWARE: Rhinoceros, Alphacam
MATERIAL: Birch plywood
FABRICATION: 2D CNC profile cuts
Funded by the Georgia Institute of Technology Thomas W.
Ventulett III Distinguished Chair in Architectural Design

A Change of State, Georgia Institute of Technology/
Nader Tehrani, 2006
DESIGNERS: Nader Tehrani (faculty), Tristan Al-Haddad
(instructor), Brandon Clifford (project lead)
TEAM: Richard Aeck, Jonathan Baker, Daniel Baron, Vishwadeep
Deo, Brandi Flanagan, Steven Georgalis, Jason Mabry,
Mohamed Mohsen, Lorraine Ong, Vinay Shiposkar
LOCATION: Georgia Institute of Technology, Atlanta, Georgia
SOFTWARE: Rhinoceros, Alphacam
MATERIAL: Polycarbonate
FABRICATION: 2D CNC profile cuts from sheet material, cold
bending on-site as a result of predrilled holes
Funded by the Georgia Institute of Technology Thomas W.
Ventulett III Distinguished Chair in Architectural Design

[c]space, Alan Dempsey and Alvin Huang, 2008
DESIGNERS: Alan Dempsey and Alvin Huang
TEAM: Patrik Schumacher, Yusuke Obuchi, Hanif Kara, Reuben
Brambleby, Jugatx Ansotegui, Oliver Bruckerman, Sawako
Kaijima, Panagiotis Michalatos, Wolfgang Rieder, Maria Pixner,
Gerhard Enn, Arnold Leiter, Bodo Röder

SITE TEAM: Design Research Laboratory
João Bravo da Costa, Alkis Dikaios, Aditya Chandra, Alan
Jinsoo Kim, Jwalant Mahadevwala, Rashiq Muhammad Ali,
Carlos Andres, Parraga Botero, Thomas Andres Jacobsen-
Collado, Pierandrea Angius, Saif Ala'a Al-Masri, Abhishek Bij,
Rochana Chaugule, Rafael Contreras Morales, Xia Chun, Kai
Chun Hu, Claudia Dorner, Pavlos Fereos, Brian Houghton,
Julian Jones, Shipra Narang, Iain (Max) Maxwell, Sergio, Reyes
Rodriguez, Diego Ricalde Recchia, Alexander Robles Palacio,
Ujjal Roy, Rajat Sodhi
LOCATION: Architectural Association, London, U.K.
SOFTWARE: Rhinoceros, AutoCAD
MATERIALS: Fiber-reinforced concrete, steel
FABRICATION: CNC water-jet cutter, CNC plasma cutter

BURST*.003, SYSTEMarchitects, 2006
DESIGNERS: Douglas Gauthier, Jeremy Edmiston
TEAM: Sarkis Arakelyan, Amber Lynn Bard, Ayat Fadaifard,
Sara Goldsmith, Henry Grosman, Kobi Jakov, Joseph Jelinek,
Ginny Hyo-jin Kang, Gen Kato, Yarek Karawczyk, Ioanna
Karagiannakou, Tony Su
ENGINEER: Buro Happold
CONSULTING ENGINEERS: Craig Schwitter (partner), Cristobal
Correa (structural engineer), Byron Stigge (mechanical engineer)
LOCATION: North Haven, Australia
SOFTWARE: form•Z, VectorWorks, StringIT
MATERIALS: Plywood, wood decking, painted steel, painted
expanded metal, door and window hardware, galvanized-metal
flashing, bolts, screws, poured-resin flooring, paint, sealant,
Bondo finish, Vulkem waterproofing membrane, concrete
foundation footings, insulated glass, incandescent light fixtures
FABRICATION: Laser cutter, CNC router

Tessellating

West Coast Pavilion, Atelier Manferdini, 2006
DESIGNER: Elena Manferdini
TEAM: Jae Rodriguez, Midori Mizuhara
LOCATION: Architectural Biennial Beijing 2006, Beijing, China
SOFTWARE: Maya
MATERIALS: Wood and styrene
FABRICATION: CNC laser cutter, CNC mill

Huyghe + Le Corbusier Puppet Theater, MOS, 2004
DESIGNERS: Michael Meredith, Hilary Sample
TEAM: Harvard Graduate School of Design students Geoff von
Oeyen, Chad Burke, Zac Culbreth, Elliot Hodges, Fred Holt
LOCATION: Carpenter Center for the Visual Arts, Harvard
University, Cambridge, Massachusetts
MATERIALS: Polycarbonate panels, urethane foam, moss
FABRICATION: Heat forming, CNC mill

Helios House, Office dA and Johnston Marklee & Associates,
2006–7
DESIGNERS: Office dA and Johnston Marklee & Associates
Office dA: Nader Tehrani, Monica Ponce de Leon; Office dA

team: Dan Gallagher, Arthur Chang, Christian Ervin, Lisa Huang, Ji-Young Park, Brandon Clifford, Cathlyn Newell, Harry Lowd; Johnston Marklee & Associates: Sharon Johnston, Mark Lee; Johnston Marklee team: Anne Rosenberg, Robert Garlipp, Lorena Yamamoto
MATERIALS: Vibration-finish stainless steel, fiberglass substructure (canopy)
FABRICATION: Laser cutter, 3D CNC profile cutter

California: Stage Set for John Jasperse,
AEDS/Ammar Eloueini, 2003
DESIGNER: Ammar Eloueini
TEAM: Gonçalo Antunes de Azevedoeorgia
LOCATION: Festival International de Dance, Cannes, France, and later performed internationally
SOFTWARE: Softimage XSI, Pepakura Designer, AutoCAD
MATERIAL: Polycarbonate
FABRICATION: CNC router

Airspace Tokyo, Thom Faulders Architecture, 2007
SCREEN-FACADE DESIGN: Thom Faulders Architecture, with Sean Ahlquist/PROCES2
SCREEN-FACADE DESIGN TEAM: Thom Faulders, Sean Ahlquist, Hajime Masubuchi, Patrick Flynn, Jessica Kmetovic, Tomohiko Sakai, Agnessa Torodova
BUILDING DESIGN: Hajime Masubuchi/Studio M (Tokyo)
LOCATION: Tokyo, Japan
SOFTWARE: 3D Studio Max, GenerativeComponents, VectorWorks
MATERIALS: Aluminum and plastic composite, stainless-steel rods, aluminum brackets
FABRICATION: Hand-cut from full-scale digital plots as templates

Technicolor Bloom, Brennan Buck, 2007
DESIGNERS: Brennan Buck, with Rob Henderson
TEAM: Dumene Comploi, Elizabeth Brauner, Eva Diem, Manfred Herman, Maja Ozvaldic, Anna Psenicka, Bika Rebek
LOCATION: Sliver Gallery, Vienna, Austria
SOFTWARE: Maya
MATERIALS: 5-mm plywood, paint, plastic zip ties
FABRICATION: 2½-axis CNC cutter

Folding

Dragonfly, Tom Wiscombe/EMERGENT, 2007
DESIGNERS: Tom Wiscombe/EMERGENT and Buro Happold; EMERGENT team: Kevin Regalado, John Hoffman, Dionicio Valdez
ENGINEERING TEAM: Greg Otto, Matt Melnyk, Steve Boak, Ricardo Carrillo
ERECTION: Hinerfeld-Ward, Tom Hinerfeld
LOCATION: SCI-Arc Gallery, Los Angeles
MATERIAL: ⅛-inch aluminum
FABRICATION: Three-axis CNC mill

Nubik, AEDS/Ammar Eloueini, 2005
DESIGNER: Ammar Eloueini/AEDS
TEAM: Marcin Szef

LOCATION: Grand Arts, Kansas City, Missouri
SOFTWARE: Softimage XSI, Pepakura Design, AutoCAD
MATERIAL: Polycarbonate
FABRICATION: CNC router

In-Out Curtain, IwamotoScott, 2005
DESIGNERS: Lisa Iwamoto, Craig Scott
TEAM: Beau Trincia, Emily Gosack
MATERIAL: Lenderink Paperwood
FABRICATION: Laser cutter

Entry Paradise Pavilion, Chris Bosse/PTW Architects, 2006
DESIGNER: Chris Bosse/PTW Architects
LOCATION: Zollverein, Essen, Germany
SOFTWARE: "Taiyo membranes" used at Taiyo membranes
MATERIALS: Specially treated high-tech Nylon and light
FABRICATION: Laser cutter with 5-m table

Aoba-tei, Atelier Hitoshi Abe, 2004
DESIGNER: Hitoshi Abe
TEAM: Naoki Inada, Yasuyuki Sakuma
LOCATION: Sendai, Japan
SOFTWARE: VectorWorks, Photoshop, Illustrator
MATERIALS: 2.3-mm steel plate, water-based urethane with ceramic powder
FABRICATION: CNC turret

Digital Origami, University of Technology, Sydney/ Chris Bosse, 2007
DESIGNERS: University of Technology, Sydney, master-class students, Chris Bosse (faculty)
LOCATION: Sydney, Australia
MATERIAL: Recycled cardboard
FABRICATION: Laser cutter

C_Wall, Andrew Kudless/Matsysa, 2006
DESIGNER: Andrew Kudless/Matsys
TEAM: Ivan Vukcevich, Ronnie Parsons, Zak Snider, Austin Poe, Camie Vacha, Cassie Matthys, Christopher Friend, Nicholas Cesare, Anthony Rodriguez, Mark Wendell, Joel Burke, Brandon Hendrick, Chung-tzu Yeh, Doug Stechschultze, Gene Shevchenko, Kyu Chun, Nick Munoz, Sabrina Sierawski
LOCATION: Banvard Gallery, Knowlton School of Architecture, Ohio State University
SOFTWARE: Rhinoceros, RhinoScript, Qhull
MATERIAL: Two-ply museum board
FABRICATION: Laser cutter, folding

Manifold, Andrew Kudless, 2004
DESIGNER: Andrew Kudless/Matsys
TEAM: Jayendra Sha, Nikolaos Stathopoulos, Giorgos Kailis, Matthew Johnson, Ranidia Lemon, Muchuan Xu, Grace Li, Scott Cahill, Wongpat Suetrong
LOCATION: Architectural Association, London
SOFTWARE: Maya MEL script, Rhinoceros, form•Z, AutoCAD
MATERIAL: 3-mm solid cardboard
FABRICATION: Laser cutter, folding

Contouring

Bone Wall, Urban A&O, 2006
DESIGNER: Joe MacDonald
PROJECT CAPTAINS: Andrew Atwood, Landon Brown, Todd Shafer, Erik Tietz
TEAM: Behrang Behin, Jef Czekaj, Darby Foreman, Teddy Huyck, Christoph Ibele, Christopher Parlato, Cameo Roehrich, Christopher Ryan, Suzannah Sinclair, Timothy Talun, Daniel Kiss
LOCATION: Storefront for Art and Architecture, New York
SOFTWARE: CATIA V5R17
MATERIAL: High-density foam
FABRICATION: CNC mill

Design 306, Erwin Hauer and Enrique Rosado, 2005
DESIGNERS: Erwin Hauer and Enrique Rosado
LOCATION: Rockefeller Center, New York
SOFTWARE: Rhinoceros
MATERIALS: Indiana limestone, MDF
FABRICATION: Three-axis CNC mill, Digital Stone Project (fabricators)

CNC Panels, Jeremy Ficca, 2004
DESIGNER: Jeremy Ficca
SOFTWARE: AutoCAD, VisualMill
MATERIAL: Seven-ply Baltic-birch plywood
FABRICATION: Three-axis CNC mill

Door with Peephole, WILLIAMSONWILLIAMSON, 2004
DESIGNERS: Betsy Williamson and Shane Williamson
LOCATION: Mercer Union Gallery, Toronto
SOFTWARE: Rhinoceros, ThinkDesign, Mastercam
MATERIAL: Aviation plywood
FABRICATION: Three-axis CNC mill

Gradient Scale, SPAN, 2005
DESIGNERS: Matias del Campo and Sandra Manninger
TEAM: Manfred Hermann, Rob Henderson, Thomas Aigelsreiter, Philipp Müller, Friedrich Biedermann
LOCATION: Zumtobel Lightforum, Vienna, Austria
SOFTWARE: Maya, Rhinoceros, SURFCAM
MATERIALS: Extruded polystyrene, polyurethane coating, interference paint
FABRICATION: Three-axis mill

Tool-Hide, Ruy Klein, 2006
DESIGNERS: David Ruy, Karel Klein
SOFTWARE: Maya, MasterCAM
MATERIALS: MDF, metallic pearl paint, clear coat
FABRICATION: CNC mill, Associated Fabrication, Brooklyn

Forming

Alice, Florencia Pita mod, 2007
DESIGNER: Florencia Pita
TEAM: Tanja Werner, Guillermina Chiu, Ai Amano, Jerry Figurski, McCall Holman
LOCATION: LAXART GALLERY, Culver City, California

SOFTWARE: Maya, Rhinoceros, SURFCAM
MATERIALS: Cast urethane, orange pigment, eighth-inch-thick PETG, orange vinyl, high-density sheet Polyfoam, MDF, styrene
FABRICATION: CNC mill, vacuum forming, casting, laminating

Prototype pavilion, MOS, 2005
DESIGNERS: Michael Meredith, Hilary Sample
TEAM: Chad Burke, Elliot Hodges, Fred Holt
LOCATION: Unknown
SOFTWARE: Maya, Rhinoceros, SURFCAM
MATERIALS: Fiberglass, urethane foam, galvanized steel
FABRICATION: Plasma cutter, CNC mill

UniBodies, PATTERNS, with Kreysler & Associates, 2006
DESIGNERS: Marcelo Spina and Makai Smith; PATTERNS team: Georgina Huljich, Seyavash Zohoori, Marcus Friesl, Jooyoung Chun; Kreysler & Associates team: Scott Van Note, Joshua Zabel, Jesus Ambriz-Villasenor, Miguel Ambriz-Villasenor, Jesus Flores
LOCATION: Artists Space, New York
SOFTWARE: Maya, Rhinoceros
MATERIALS: In-mold and post-applied FRP, aluminum, stainless steel, various plastic finishes
FABRICATION: Composite lamination of fiberglass over CNC-milled urethane molds

NGTV, GNUFORM, 2005
DESIGNERS: Jason Payne and Heather Roberge
TEAM: Tim Gorter, Adam Fure, Kelly Bair
LOCATION: No Good Television Headquarters, Beverly Hills, California
SOFTWARE: Maya, Rhinoceros, AutoCAD
MATERIALS: Eighth-inch PETG, LED lighting, 1977 Porche Red automotive paint, eighth-inch black rubber, crimson synthetic fur, body-piercing hardware, plywood substructure
FABRICATION: CNC mill, vacuum forming, analog upholstering, combing and styling (of fur)

"Dark Places," servo, 2006
DESIGNERS: David Erdman, Chris Perry, Marcelyn Gow
TEAM: Mike Hill, Jeremy Whitener, Ellie Abrons, Kim Watts
LOCATION: Santa Monica Museum of Art, Santa Monica, California
SOFTWARE: Rhinoceros, SURFCAM
MATERIALS: PETG, aluminum
FABRICATION: Vacuum forming

"Housing in Vienna," SPAN, 2007–8
DESIGNERS: Matias del Campo and Sandra Manninger
TEAM: Alexandra Viehhauser, Günther Dreger, Gerold Kubischeck, Günther Kellner, Philipp Aschenberger, Heinz Ortmayr
LOCATION: Traveling exhibition by the Architecture Center Vienna
SOFTWARE: TopMod, Maya, Rhinoceros, SURFCAM
MATERIAL: PETG
FABRICATION: Three-axis mill, vacuum forming

Satin Sheet, University of California, Los Angeles/
Heather Roberge, 2007
DESIGNERS: Heather Roberge (faculty), Miguel Alvarez, Daniel
Carper, Alissa Hisoire, Carrie Smith
TEAM: Miguel Alvarez, Daniel Carper, Alissa Hisoire, Carrie Smith
LOCATION: Perloff Hall, UCLA, Los Angeles, California
SOFTWARE: Rhinoceros, SURFCAM, Illustrator
MATERIALS: Urethane foam, ABS sheet, PETG sheets,
diachromatic paint
FABRICATION: CNC mill, vacuum forming, airbrush

Shiatsu, University of California, Los Angeles/
Heather Roberge, 2007
DESIGNERS: Heather Roberge (faculty), Michael Ben-Meir,
Kyle Miller, Marcin Szef
TEAM: Michael Ben-Meir, Kyle Miller, Marcin Szef
LOCATION: Perloff Hall, UCLA, Los Angeles, California
SOFTWARE: Rhinoceros, SURFCAM, Illustrator
MATERIAL: PETG sheets
FABRICATION: Drape forming, air brushing

P_Wall, Andrew Kudless/Matsys, 2006
DESIGNER: Andrew Kudless/Matsys
TEAM: Ivan Vukcevich, Kyu Chun, Ryan Palider
LOCATION: Banvard Gallery, Knowlton School of Architecture,
Ohio State University
SOFTWARE: Rhinoceros, RhinoScript
MATERIALS: Plaster, Lycra
FABRICATION: Flexible fabric formwork from digitally derived
point locations